New York & New Jersey

HENRY C. KEATTS

Pisces Books
A division of Gulf Publishing Company
Houston, Texas

Dedication

To my sons, Tim, Chris, and Shawn

Pisces Books
A division of Gulf Publishing Company
P.O. Box 2608
Houston, Texas 77252-2608

Library of Congress Cataloging-in-Publication Data

Keatts, Henry.
    Guide to shipwreck diving. New York & New Jersey / Henry C. Keatts.
        p.   cm.
    Includes index.
    ISBN 1-55992-056-4
    1. Scuba diving—New York. 2. Scuba diving—New Jersey.
3. Shipwrecks—New York. 4. Shipwrecks—New Jersey. I. Title.
GV840.S78K33   1992
797.2'3—dc20   91-34525
                                                              CIP

Printed and bound in the United States of America
(Color pages printed in Hong Kong)

10   9   8   7   6   5   4   3   2   1

Table of Contents

Acknowledgments

Without the contributions and cooperation of the following individuals and organizations, this book would not have been possible:

Val Ackins
Joe Bereswill
Steve Bielenda
Kevin Brennan
Mike Colasurdo
Charles Cole
Tim Coleman
Chip Cooper
Bill Davis
Mike deCamp
Bill deMarigny
Steve Gatto
Aaron Hirsch
George Hoffman
Al Hofmann
Jon Hulburt
Howard Klein

John Lachenmeyer
Dan Lieb
Bart Malone
Greg Modelle
Pete Nawrocky
Tom Packer
Frank Persico
Julius Pignataro
George Power
George Quirk
Bill Reddan
Tom Roach
Bill Schmoldt
Brian Skerry
Brad Sheard
Rich Taracka

The Mariners' Museum
The Peabody Museum of Salem
Steamship Historical Society
University of Baltimore Library
Society for the Preservation of New England Antiquities
Dossin Great Lakes Museum
Suffolk County Marine Museum
Suffolk County Historical Society
National Archives
Naval Historical Center

Special thanks are due to George Farr for his editorial assistance, and to Viking Diving Division for the use of their excellent diving suits and Poseidon regulators.

Preface

The divers who frequent the New York Bight and Long Island Sound enjoy the best and most unique diving in the United States. They have access to history under the sea in the shape of the ships of war, commerce, and transportation that have been lost in those waters since before the Pilgrims set foot on Plymouth Rock. New York City owes its beginnings to the trade enterprise of the Dutch. Their founding of New Amsterdam in 1624 led to a steady growth of commerce until New York became the commercial capital of the New World, then the entire world.

A continuing flow of merchant vessels has linked metropolitan New York with exotic ports of call around the globe. Prior to the Civil War all great American fortunes stemmed from the sea. Ships and shipping were the most conspicuous features of New York business life, with the waterfront the city's focal point of interest and activity.

The first recorded local shipwreck was Adriaen Block's *Tiger* in 1614. The Dutch ship caught fire while at anchor off Manhattan Island. Hundreds of vessels of all types have sunk off New York and New Jersey since then — victims of winter storms, dense fog, fire, military conflict, and human error.

During both world wars, German U-boats crossed the Atlantic to prey upon merchant and naval vessels in American waters. Nine ships covered in this book were sunk by U-boats.

There are far too many shipwrecks off the coasts of New York and New Jersey for all of them to be covered in this book. A guideline that no wrecks in more than 130 feet of water be included was established. Most of the wrecks that are described are popular dive spots visited by many sport divers each year.

Familiarity with a ship's history adds a new dimension of interest to the exploration of its remains. This volume provides the background of each vessel and a description of its present condition.

Many equate wreck diving with treasure hunting. The latter enjoys universal appeal, but is usually unrewarding if the search is for gold, silver, or jewels. For the most part, divers are rewarded with more commonplace relics, or *artifacts*. The word artifact comes from the Latin *arte factum*, meaning something made with skill. Artifacts, too, are treasures — treasures in, and of, history.

Wreck diving has fostered archaeological and historical marine research. It has also enabled the collection of rare artifacts from vessels that have rested at the bottom of the sea for decades, even centuries. The

v

recovery, identification, dating, and preservation of those historical objects attract both amateur and professional archaeologists. Preservation is the moral responsibility of a diver who removes a relic from a sunken ship. Individual sport divers have repeatedly displayed their ability to restore historical artifacts, but the techniques of restoration and preservation are complicated, time-consuming, and costly. Marine artifact exhibits at museums, historical societies, and dive symposiums have been instrumental in educating the public in the maritime history of this nation.

There is some controversy regarding the charge that sport divers are "ripping off" historical wrecks. Except for a few wrecks located in relatively protected areas, all wrecks are being destroyed slowly but surely (along with their artifacts) for all time. The sea is cruel to all that does not belong in it. Even steel hulls cannot withstand the combined forces of winds, waves, currents, and corrosion.

A word to the wise: *the passage of HR74, the abandoned shipwreck bill, has given individual states the sovereignty to determine and interpret the status of all shipwrecks submerged in state waters. Divers should watch for ongoing developments resulting in increased clarification of this legislation.*

One imperative has dictated the preparation of this book, and that is historical accuracy. Historical accuracy has been pursued to the fullest possible extent. If you, the reader, note an inaccuracy or misinterpretation, or if you find information missing, I would welcome your input. Information, photographs, and slides forwarded to Professor Henry C. Keatts, Suffolk Community College, Riverhead, NY 11901, will receive appreciative attention and confirming research for inclusion in further editions of this work.

Henry C. Keatts
East Moriches, NY

1

Local Conditions

Equipment. At least a full wetsuit, hood, boots, and gloves are needed to dive the waters off the coast of New York and New Jersey. A buoyancy compensator, depth gauge, bottom timer, dive computer, sharp knife, light (two lights if the diver plans to penetrate a wreck), and penetration/tether line are also useful equipment to bring along. An adequate air supply should include a backup system, such as a pony bottle or double tanks with separate regulators, especially if penetration is planned.

Season. For most divers, May through the middle of October is the prime time to dive these waters. However, some dive charter boats start in March and run until November. George Hoffman, captain and owner of *Sea Lion*, out of Manasquan Inlet, NJ, runs year round. The water temperatures range from the low 30s in February and March to the mid-70s in mid-July to mid-September.

Visibility. The ability to see underwater in this area is as unpredictable as the weather. Divers seldom agree on visibility; one will claim that it is ten feet and the next diver to surface will say 40 feet. This much is sure: excellent visibility is seldom encountered in northeast waters, and 30 feet is considered good. Visibility is usually better when the bottom is sand because light is reflected. A mud and silt bottom absorbs light and can be easily disturbed by a diver, surge, or current, further reducing visibility.

An average visibility is provided for each wreck in this book, but many will disagree with these figures because of the extreme variability of visibility on northeast shipwrecks — from a few inches to more than 50 feet.

Marine Life. In the absence of natural reefs in the northeast, it is interesting that man, albeit unintentionally, has provided the basis for fascinating ecosystems: shipwrecks. They provide large areas of hard surface for colonizing marine organisms, and after a few years each wreck is an entire ecosystem. They are not only oases in a desert of sand, but they also increase biologic productivity. It is stunning to see for the

1

first time the incredible abundance, beauty, and diversity of marine life that has taken up residence in or around a sunken ship. On some wrecks, the growth of marine organisms is so dense that it completely obscures the structures of the vessel.

New York requires residents and out-of-state divers to have a license to catch lobsters. Such a permit can be obtained from the Department of Environmental Conservation, Bldg. 40, SUNY, Stony Brook, NY 11794. Most New York dive charter boats purchase a commercial license that covers all passengers. New Jersey does not require a license regardless of residency. In both states, lobsters must measure at least 3³⁄₁₆ inches from the eye socket to the end of the carapace, and must not bear eggs.

Hazards. Shipwrecks are often beautiful and always fascinating for the sport diver; however, they may be hazardous. The entangling monofilament of lost fishing lines and nets are constant hazards for wreck divers. It is the main reason for carrying a sharp knife. Penetrating wrecks, especially deep ones, can also be hazardous, and divers need to observe certain safety rules. Even if ambient light is available, disturbed silt and oxidation from rusting metal will reduce visibility. A wreck diving course that teaches penetration (some do not) or a cave diving course is recommended before divers attempt penetrating a shipwreck. Dives requiring decompression stops add complications and hazard.

Disorientation on large wrecks, especially ones with scattered wreckage, can make it difficult for a diver to return to the anchor line. Ascending without the anchor line in a strong current can leave a diver facing an exhausting swim back to the boat. Another hazard in surfacing away from the dive boat is the possibility of being struck by another vessel. Attaching a tether line to the anchor chain and paying attention to landmarks decreases the risk. Remember, a tether line may be cut by wreckage or another diver who has become entangled in it. If a penetration/tether line is used, it is important to reel the line in. Left in or outside a wreck, the line becomes a potential entangling hazard. Tidal fluctuations that can produce strong currents present another potential hazard.

Even shallow wrecks may be hazardous. Waves breaking over and around inshore wrecks can create a surge that will alternately push and pull. The sudden loss of control can throw a diver into jagged metal or other harmful objects. Such diving is especially hazardous when visibility is poor.

Wreck diving can be safe with proper training, equipment, and procedures. It should not be attempted without thorough professional preparation. Wreck diving certification is not required by dive charter boats, but basic certification is. However, wreck diving is no place for a beginning diver. Inexperienced divers should register for a wreck diving certification course through a dive shop. Even after completing the course, the diver should proceed in graduated steps to the deeper, more hazardous wrecks.

Loran Numbers. Loran [Lo(ng) ra(nge) n(avigation)] is a long-range navigational system that uses pulsed radio signals from two or more pairs of ground stations of known position. A navigator uses the signals to establish his own position. Accuracy of the Loran numbers listed in this book depend on the sensitivity of the individual units and the operator's ability to use the apparatus. When Loran numbers are obtained from one unit and used on another, they may not be accurate and should be considered a starting point for finding a shipwreck.

Some of the Loran numbers listed in this volume have been obtained from more than one source; if they differed, both have been listed. The difference could be due to the sensitivity of the two machines, or the numbers could be for different parts of the wreck. Some shipwrecks such as the armored cruiser *San Diego* are very large, and the Loran numbers will vary from bow to stern.

Familiarity with the use of a depth recorder and the interpretation of its readings is very important in finding a shipwreck.

Dive ratings. The skill level the diver should possess is listed in the heading for each wreck. Some shipwrecks will have multiple ratings because of varying conditions. It is highly recommended that a diver be certified on the advanced open water and wreck diving level before visiting any of these shipwrecks. The ratings are as follows:

Novice. Wreck diving certification with little or no wreck diving experience. Novice wreck divers should do no penetrations and limit their depths to 40 feet.

Intermediate. Wreck diving certification with a moderate amount of wreck diving experience. Intermediate wreck divers should only practice limited penetration when ambient light is available and little silt is within the penetration area. Depth should be limited to 80 feet.

Advanced. Wreck diving certification and extensive wreck diving experience. Advanced wreck divers should be very experienced in all aspects of penetration at depths up to 130 feet. Dives become more hazardous when divers overestimate their abilities.

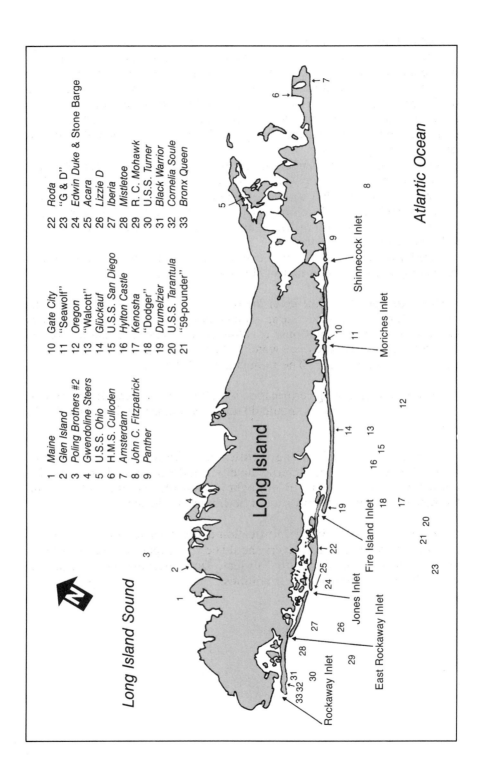

Long Island Sound

Long Island

Atlantic Ocean

1 Maine
2 Glen Island
3 Poling Brothers #2
4 Gwendoline Steers
5 U.S.S. Ohio
6 H.M.S. Culloden
7 Amsterdam
8 John C. Fitzpatrick
9 Panther

10 Gate City
11 "Seawolf"
12 Oregon
13 "Walcott"
14 Glückauf
15 U.S.S. San Diego
16 Hylton Castle
17 Kenosha
18 "Dodger"
19 Drumelzier
20 U.S.S. Tarantula
21 "59-pounder"

22 Roda
23 "G & D"
24 Edwin Duke & Stone Barge
25 Acara
26 Lizzie D
27 Iberia
28 Mistletoe
29 R. C. Mohawk
30 U.S.S. Turner
31 Black Warrior
32 Cornelia Soule
33 Bronx Queen

Shinnecock Inlet

Moriches Inlet

Fire Island Inlet

Jones Inlet

East Rockaway Inlet

Rockaway Inlet

New York Shipwrecks

Maine

Approximate depth: 15'
Average visibility: 5'
Expertise: Novice to advanced
depending on visibility, current,
and boat traffic
Current/surge: None to strong
Bottom: Rocks, silt, and sand
Location: 100 yards northeast of
Execution Rocks Lighthouse

Loran numbers: 26938.5 43937.8
Launched: 1891
Sunk: February 4, 1920
Cause: Pack ice
Type: Passenger liner
Length/beam: 310'/44'
Tonnage: 1,505
Condition: Scattered wreckage

History. In the days before the American Revolution, Colonial unrest plagued the British so unbearably that harsh measures were instituted to discourage the colonists from acts against the Crown. Public executions terminated the actions of perpetrators, but their last shouts of defiant rebellion against the King added resolve to the growing resistance of Colonial onlookers.

A reef known as Cow Neck, between the Port of New York and Long Island Sound, about one mile off Sands Point, Long Island, NY, was chosen to serve as the site for executions. As it was far removed from population centers, executions could be conducted without public observation. A pit was dug in the reef, and iron rings were firmly fastened into the adjacent rocks. At low tide, condemned prisoners were chained to the rings and left to drown with the rising tide, without an audience. The site became known as "Execution Rocks."

A lighthouse was constructed on the site in 1849 to warn Long Island steamers away from the treacherous approach to New York City, and Congress declared that never again would any man feel "chained" to Execution Rocks. Keepers of other lighthouses were required to serve for a specific time, but any Execution Rocks keeper who felt uncomfortable with the "ghosts" of the past could be "honourably" transferred "without prejudice."

The steamer Maine. *Courtesy of the Steamship Historical Society Collection, University of Baltimore Library.*

The new Providence and Stonington Line steel-hulled steamer *Maine* was the first screw-propeller passenger ship to be placed in service on the Sound by one of the major lines. She was launched in 1891, 42 years after the lighthouse was constructed, and was about 30 percent more economical to operate than the old-style paddle wheelers. The 310-foot-long steamer had a 44-foot beam, but she was fast. *Maine* reached a speed of 17.6 knots on her first run.

The new vessel carried a crew of 70 and was equipped with 106 staterooms that could accommodate 500 passengers. The passenger entrance led to an elegantly fitted social hall. The grand stairway led to the 243-foot-long main saloon, which was decorated in ivory with gold leaf and large mirrors. Light was filtered from above through two beautiful cupolas. Coats of arms adorned the stairway leading to the upper-deck dining saloon. There, three decks high, passengers could take their meals while viewing the passing scene.

Maine's maiden voyage was March 12, 1892. For the next 28 years she carried passengers and cargo from New York City to Bridgeport, Stonington, Providence, Fall River, and other New England ports. By February 1920 the steamer was serving as a winter relief ship on the Bridgeport Line of the New England Steamship Co.

During winter months the waters of Long Island Sound were often clogged with ice floes. Sailing vessels frequently required assistance or rescue from the ice by steamers. The winter of 1919-1920 was particularly harsh; many steamers were trapped in the ice, as if they were in the arctic rather than almost in sight of the towers of Manhattan. *Maine*'s Chief Engineer Charles Pierce later stated that it was the toughest winter he had ever put in, and he was a veteran of 50 winters on the Sound.

Sinking. On the afternoon of February 4, 1920, *Maine*, with a full cargo but only a few passengers, left her East River pier for Bridgeport in company with several other steamers. Bucking heavy ice floes, with her steel prow cutting through heavily packed ice, she worked out of the East River into Long Island Sound, where a northeast blizzard was driving the Sound ice into great jams. The steamers became trapped in the four-foot-thick pieces of ice off Execution Rocks.

As the weather worsened, gale-force wind and flood tide carried the ice-trapped *Maine* toward Execution Rocks. The steamer struck stern first, puncturing her hull in the shaft alley. The ice movement swung her around and another rock opened her bottom under the boiler room, flooding that compartment. The steamer had seven watertight compartments, but a coal shovel had washed under the watertight bulkhead door leading to the engine room just as it was closing. The door jammed partially open, flooding that compartment as well. The steamer settled to the bottom, with water above the freight deck.

Chief Engineer Pierce recalled, "We had only a few emergency lights. . . . We wondered if we would ever get off. Fortunately there were only a few passengers. Some of them took it hard." The creaking, snapping, and crushing of ice against the steamer's steel hull frightened both crew and passengers. Pierce continued, "It sounded like Fourth of July but didn't feel like it. . . . We were there three nights and three days before they could get to us. It seemed like three months. Our drinking water ran out. We shoveled snow off the top deck and melted it in order to have something to drink. Our food ran so low we really got scared."

A steamer managed to work through the thinning ice and removed the passengers. Food and water were left for *Maine*'s crew.

Maine proved to be the only steamer that had grounded; as the ice pack thinned, the other steamers freed themselves. A survey of the sunken ship revealed that in addition to the two hull punctures that were made when she struck the rocks, an open crack in her starboard side extended from bilge to gunwale.

The Dive. The wreck is located in about 15 feet of water, but only scattered steel I-beams and hull plates remain. Some pieces extend several feet off the bottom.

Although a wreck symbol shows *Maine*'s location on nautical charts, it can be difficult to locate because of the large rocks that sent her to the bottom. There is heavy small-boat traffic in the area; their operators either do not know what a dive flag represents or they do not care. Divers must come back up the anchor line, but poor to bad visibility makes it difficult to do so. A tether line should be tied to the anchor line to ensure finding it at the end of a dive. It is safer to dive the wreck on a weekday to avoid heavy weekend boat traffic, and to dive at slack high tide to reduce an often strong current and improve visibility.

After the salvors left, Maine*'s hulk awaits the end, above. Below, the steamer is ablaze from stem to stern. Courtesy of The Mariners' Museum, Newport News, VA.*

Artifacts. After the steamer grounded, the crew stripped the wreck. Dishes, silverware, and other galley equipment were checked against the inventory; any excess was dropped over the side. Only what was supposed to be on board was returned to the line's headquarters at Newport.

A salvage company removed the helm, whistle, bell, lifeboat davits, stateroom fixtures, lighting fixtures, dining and saloon furniture, and even the beautiful butternut paneling that adorned the walls of the bridal suite. The engine was removed, but the four boilers, shaft, and single screw-propeller were not deemed worth the salvage effort.

After the salvage work was completed, the old steamer was burned to the waterline.

In a 1980 dive, bronze porthole rims were recovered; several more and other bronze artifacts were in view, but those artifacts have since been removed.

Approximate depth: 15'
Average visibility: 5'
Expertise required: Novice
Current/surge: None to moderate
Bottom: Sand, silt, and rocks
Location: About 100 yards off-shore, between Matinecock Point and Glen Cove, NY
Loran numbers: 26893.6 43937.6
Launched: 1880

Sunk: December 17, 1904
Cause: Fire
Type: Side-paddle wheel passenger liner
Length/beam: 238.9'/35.8'
Tonnage: 615
Condition: The hull extends about two feet above the bottom; scattered wreckage

History. In many maritime disasters the "black gang," firemen and stokers from below, are accused of being among the first to abandon ship. Those soot-and-coal-dust-covered crewmen are reputed to leave a doomed ship without consideration for the vessel's passengers. That did not apply when the Starin Line side-paddle wheeler *Glen Island* burned and sank in 1904.

Thirteen years earlier, the steamer, then named *City of Richmond* and owned by the Hartford Line, had been badly damaged by fire. The Starin Line bought and rebuilt her as a summer excursion steamer. During summer months the 24-year-old steamer, renamed *Glen Island*, functioned as an excursion vessel ferrying passengers between New York City and Glen Island, Long Island. During winter months she served as a relief ship on Starin's New Haven route, primarily a freight run with only a few passengers.

Sinking. On December 17, 1904, *Glen Island*, carrying cargo and only 10 passengers, was en route to New Haven. She had passed Glen Island, her summer port of call, just after midnight, and was about two miles

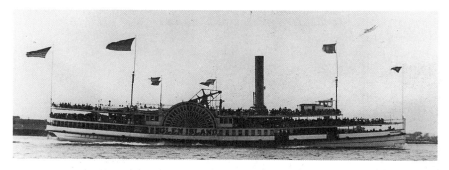

The steamer Glen Island *burned and sank off the north shore of Long Island. Courtesy of The Mariners' Museum, Newport News, VA.*

off the Connecticut shore. Pilot Thomas McMullin and Quartermaster John O'Brien were in the pilothouse when the electric lights failed. McMullin stayed at the wheel but two minutes later he lost steering. As he and O'Brien struggled at the wheel, the fire-alarm bell began to ring. McMullin dashed out of the pilothouse in response to the alarm, and was met by a cloud of smoke rolling through the upper saloon. Captain Charles E. MacAllister was already on deck calling his crew to quarters.

Flames that had started below decks about midships had already reached the cargo of Christmas gifts and barrels of oil and whiskey. Within five minutes nine persons died in the rapidly spreading blaze and dense smoke.

Captain MacAllister realized his command was doomed; he quickly ordered the abandon-ship alarm to be rung and the lifeboats unshipped. Passengers awakened by the alarm had to grope in total darkness for clothing, and then were led to the lifeboats by crew members. MacAllister ordered "Women first"; there were no children on board. One terror-stricken male passenger rushed forward but was discouraged by a blow that sent him reeling backward. The women were handed down into the first boat.

One male and one female passenger were among the nine casualties. Mrs. Rosa Silken of New Haven had left her stateroom and was being led to the deck by a stewardess when she remembered her money and jewelry that she had left behind. She dashed back after them. As the second lifeboat was filling, the woman had not reappeared. Fireman Newman Miller went below to search for her. By that time wooden-hulled *Glen Island* was a roaring furnace; both Miller and Mrs. Silken perished.

Hundreds watched the blazing steamer from the Connecticut and Long Island shores and wondered which of the Sound's fleet was perishing before their eyes.

An east-bound tug cast off her tow, steamed over, and rescued the eight passengers and 14 crew members from the two lifeboats. *Glen Island* drifted across the Sound and grounded in her final resting place, off Glen Cove, NY, where she burned to the waterline.

The fire had started in the ship's galley. Its rapid spread claimed 29 percent of the 31 people on board. The same kind of accident in the

Glen Island*'s wreckage lies off the shore of this stone mansion. Photo by the author.*

Bronze ship's fastenings are embedded in wood planks and beams. Photo by the author.

summer, when *Glen Island* carried as many as 2,000 passengers, would have resulted in hundreds of deaths.

The Dive. The steamer lies in about 15 feet of water approximately 100 yards offshore from a large two-story stone mansion. All that is left of *Glen Island* is scattered wreckage and the outline of her wooden hull extending a couple of feet above the bottom. The remains of one paddle wheel can be seen lying in the sand.

Visibility is usually poor, similar to other wrecks in Long Island Sound, but there is little current with which to contend.

Artifacts. Bronze ship's fastenings are embedded in wood planks and beams, or may be found lying on top of the sand.

Beside the loss of the ship's cargo, valued at $20,000, the 10 passengers and 21 crew members lost personal belongings, including diamond studs belonging to Captain MacAllister and other jewelry.

Clay pipes and bottles are occasionally recovered.

Poling Brothers #2

Approximate depth: 65'
Average visibility: 5'
Expertise required: Advanced, due to the fishing nets and poor visibility
Current/surge: None to extreme
Bottom: Silt and mud
Location: One mile southeast of Great Captain Island

Loran numbers: 26894.8(.9) 43970.6(.7)
Launched: 1863
Sunk: February 7, 1940
Cause: Drifting ice
Type: Coastal tanker
Length/beam: 116'/23'
Tonnage: 159
Condition: Hull is intact

History and sinking. The steel-hulled coastal tanker *Poling Brothers #2*, owned by the Poling Brothers Co. of New York, was en route from New York to Cos Cob when she was lost off Great Captain Island in

Side scan sonar printout of the tanker Poling Brothers #2. Courtesy of NOAA.

western Long Island Sound. The tanker struck an ice floe and with her hull quickly filling with water her crew took to the lifeboats. A sister ship bound for Bridgeport, following *Poling Brothers #2* through the ice-cluttered waters, rescued the tanker's crew.

The 77-year-old ship had been launched in 1863 as a wooden-hulled vessel. In 1926, the 63-year-old tanker's hull was covered with steel plates.

Like others before him, Richard Taracka of the Greenwich, CT, Police Department had noticed a wreck symbol on old nautical charts, indicating a wreck was located three miles from Greenwich. Instead of speculating on what that notation might represent, he decided to try to locate the wreck. His perseverance finally paid off in 1984 when his paper-readout depth recorder showed the image he wanted — a silhouette of a shipwreck.

When Taracka and another experienced wreck diver, Bruce Mackin, head of the Norwalk, CT, Police Department's Marine Division, dived the wreck, they found it covered with fishing nets. They realized the potential danger of the nets in the typically poor visibility of the area. Since that first dive the two have painstakingly cut away most of the nets.

The divers observed rubber hoses, stenciled "fire hose," stretched across the deck, and two copper fire extinguishers lying on the deck near the pilothouse. Inside the lower level of the pilothouse, they found charred wood near a stove. A fire may have started when the tanker struck the ice floe, but did not contribute to her sinking. Hull seams had split, allowing water to enter faster than it could be expelled by the tanker's pumps.

The Dive. The tanker sits upright with her bow pointing southeasterly toward Long Island. The hull is intact, with the deck about ten feet above the bottom. The vessel has a rounded stern that is periodically covered with silt. Since her discovery, the pilothouse has been torn from the deck by a trawler's net. At the beginning of the summer, Richard Taracka puts a buoy on the wreck for the benefit of boats without Lorans.

It is important to make dives only at slack tide and to stay off the bottom. Once the silt and mud are disturbed, visibility decreases appreciably. The site is recommended only for advanced wreck divers because of the remaining nets and the poor visibility. Dive shops in New York and Connecticut offer charters to the tanker *Poling Brothers #2*.

Artifacts. The foghorn, 13 portholes, and other artifacts have been recovered. However, the ship's bell has not been found, and is probably buried in the mud. The engine room is filled with mud and has not been penetrated. By digging in the one-foot layer of silt, cage lights can be found where the pilothouse used to be.

Gwendoline Steers

Approximate depth: 45'
Average visibility: 8'
Expertise required: Advanced, due to poor visibility
Current/surge: Slight to moderate
Bottom: Silt and sand
Location: The entrance to Huntington Harbor, Long Island, NY

Loran numbers: 26798.6(.7) 43951.3(.4)
Launched: 1888
Sunk: December 30, 1962
Cause: Unknown
Type: Tug
Length/beam: 96.5'/20.6'
Tonnage: 148
Condition: Almost intact

History and sinking. On December 30, 1962, the 74-year-old iron-hulled *Gwendoline Steers* (ex. *J. Rich Steers*, ex. *Melrose*, ex. *Triton*, ex. *Douglas H. Thorne*) was on a routine trip from New York Harbor to

The body of one of the tug's crew was found frozen in a lifeboat. Courtesy of Bill Davis.

Northport, Long Island, her home port. She was scheduled to return to New York the following morning, towing barges from the Steers Sand and Gravel Co.

The day was bitterly cold and the tug was covered with sheets of ice. At 4:30 p.m., the Eatons Neck Coast Guard Station received a radio message that the tug was taking on water. Her captain reported that the pumps were handling the problem, but he would report back in an hour. The tug was not heard from again despite Coast Guard efforts to contact her. A search plane was launched in an unsuccessful attempt to find the missing tug.

The next day one of the tug's lifeboats, completely sheathed in ice, washed ashore inside Huntington Harbor. The metal hull was crushed in on both sides of the keel. The body of the tug's engineer was wedged under the front seat, frozen in a solid block of ice. Several days later two bodies washed ashore. The remaining six crewmen remained missing. So did the tugboat.

One week earlier *Gwendoline Steers* had run aground near Greenwich, CT; her hull had been repaired in a New York shipyard only days before her disappearance. It is possible that the repaired leak in her hull had opened and worsened so rapidly that the tug foundered before a radio call for assistance could be made. Did the engineer, and possibly others, have time to launch the lifeboat in which he froze to death? Did the engineer swim to the lifeboat as it broke loose and the tug went under, crushing the keel and freezing him to death? If the lifeboat *was* launched, there should have been time to flash a distress call.

For the next four months there was no indication of where the tug sank. Her location, at the entrance to Huntington Harbor, was discovered accidentally when a sailboat's keel brushed against the mast of the sunken tug. *Gwendoline Steers* had almost made it to port; she was only a couple of miles from her destination. Where she sank has been solved, but her radio silence has sealed the mystery of why.

The Dive. The wreck stands upright, but the stern is buried. The hull and wheelhouse are almost completely intact. All of the hatches and windows in the wheelhouse have been removed, making penetration easy. However, visibility is usually bad, making penetration dives more hazardous; dive lights are a must.

The wreck is covered with colorful sea anemones and northern coral. Blackfish abound and an occasional lobster can be found.

Artifacts. The most interesting artifacts, such as portholes, helm, etc., have already been recovered. Portholes, the compass, and other artifacts recovered by Ronnie Karl are on display in his restaurant, Mariner's Inn, in Northport, NY.

Approximate depth: 20'
Average visibility: 10'
Expertise required: Novice
Current/surge: Slight to moderate
Bottom: Silt and sand
Location: Greenport, NY
Launched: 1820
Sunk: April 1884

Cause: Storm
Type: Ship-of-the-line
Length/beam: 208'/53.9'
Tonnage: 2,757
Condition: Except for a few ribs, planks, and fastenings, wreckage is buried under the sand

History. In 1816, Congress authorized construction of nine ships-of-the-line, each with no fewer than 74 guns. Ships-of-the-line were the battleships of the age of sail, with armament that qualified them for position in the first line of a sea battle. They carried from 64 to more than 120 heavy cannon — floating fortresses that were a nation's most tangible symbol of sea power until they were outdated by steam power and iron hulls in the mid 1800s.

Ohio was the first of the 74s to be launched, 2½ years after her keel was laid in November 1817 at the New York Navy Yard (later Brooklyn

'U. S. SHIP OF THE LINE OHIO, *104 Guns.*

Currier and Ives lithograph of U.S.S. Ohio. *Courtesy of the Old Print Shop.*

Navy Yard). However, after her launching on May 20, 1820, she spent the next 17 years in ordinary, or "mothballed," with only a skeleton crew aboard.

In 1837, *Ohio* was sailed to the Boston Navy Yard for fitting out. The warship could carry a complement of 820, including marines. She was commissioned on October 11, 1838, and six days later sailed back to New York to be armed.

Like the others of her class, *Ohio* was designed for maximum firepower. She was nominally a 74, but carried anywhere from 84 to 104 guns, depending on the decision of her various captains. The Bureau of Ordnance Gun Register lists *Ohio*'s armament in 1845 as 90 guns.

The heavily armed ships-of-the-line posed major design problems for marine architects. They carried large numbers of heavy guns, ammunition, stores, and crew. They also had to stand up under fire. That combination called for massive dimensions and heavy armor. Yet speed and maneuverability were essential to maintain tactical superiority over enemy naval forces, and could not be sacrificed for size, armor, or armament. *Ohio* was a prime example of that refusal to compromise. During her career, the warship was acknowledged to be the Navy's best-handling and fastest ship-of-the-line. In 1850, she averaged almost 14 knots an hour for 24 hours, heading for home from Cape Horn.

For more than two years, *Ohio* patrolled the Mediterranean, leading a U.S. Navy squadron, displaying the flag and providing protection for American commerce. She returned to Boston on July 17, 1841, to spend the next five years in administrative service as a receiving ship — a floating naval depot.

War with Mexico broke out, and *Ohio* sailed to Veracruz in March 1847. She contributed to the fall of that city, not in a naval engagement,

Ohio, *although rated as a 74, carried 84 to 104 cannon, depending upon the whim of her captain. Note the Hercules figurehead on the bow. Photo from the author's collection.*

but by landing a contingent of seamen and marines equipped with ten of her guns to participate in the assault.

The large ship-of-the-line drew too much water for effective operation along the shallow coast of the Gulf of Mexico. She returned to New York in May 1847.

Ohio joined the Pacific Squadron the following year and served as a flagship for the duration of the Mexican War. When hostilities ended, the gold rush that followed the acquisition of California by the U.S. generated a boom economy on the West Coast. *Ohio* was called on to provide protection for commerce during that chaotic period. She policed the newly acquired California Territory when the Navy's major problem was to deter U.S. Navy crewmen from deserting to look for gold in the California mountains. One officer was badly mauled during an aborted attempt by two would-be deserters. A drumhead court-martial found the two guilty and sentenced them to be strung from *Ohio*'s yardarms. The bodies remained there as a grim warning to others who might otherwise have been tempted by gold.

In 1849, the warship returned to Boston. By that time, ships-of-the-line had become too costly to operate. She was decommissioned on May 3, 1850, and again went into ordinary. A year later she was recommissioned and served as a receiving ship for the next 24 years.

In 1875, *Ohio* was once more placed in ordinary, until her 63-year career ended on September 27, 1883, when she was sold to Israel L.

The old ship-of-the-line at her pier in Greenport, NY, after being sold for scrap. Courtesy of the Naval Historical Center.

Carole Keatts beside Ohio's *Hercules figurehead, now located at the village green, Stony Brook, NY. Photo by the author.*

Snow of Rockland, ME, for $17,000. Snow later sold her to Greenport, NY, shipyard owners for $20,000. Two tugs delivered her to Greenport Harbor.

Sinking. *Ohio* was moored alongside Main Street Wharf to accommodate the thousands of sightseers who, for a small fee, streamed aboard and walked the decks of the old ship-of-the-line. But it was for her copper and bronze fastenings, not display, that the warship had been purchased. Dismantling was interrupted in April 1884 by a violent storm that broke the vessel loose of her moorings and stranded her near Fanning Point at the end of Fourth Street in Greenport. She was burned to reduce her obstruction to shipping, but much of the hulk resisted the flames.

The $1,500 heroic figurehead of Hercules was removed from its place on the bow and sold at auction for $10. Later, it was resold to the owners of Canoe Place Inn, Hampton Bays, NY, for $15. In 1951, Hercules was transferred to the village green at Stony Brook, NY, where it is prominently displayed with *Ohio*'s anchor — vestiges of one of the most magnificent warships of the 19th century U.S. Navy.

Almost a century passed before extensive research by the Peconic Bay branch of the British Sub Aqua Club discovered the wreckage of *Ohio*, late in 1973.

The Dive. Some dives pose a challenge because of visibility, currents, surge, depth, conditions on a wreck, or the time one must spend on a charter boat for too little down time. *Ohio* offers a pleasant relief from

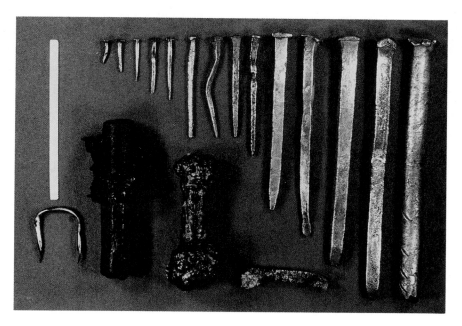

An assortment of copper, iron, and wood fastenings recovered from the wreck. Photo by the author.

such problems. The wreck rests close to shore, in Greenport Harbor. However, with very little wreckage usually exposed, the wreck can be difficult to find.

Diving from shore is favored by local divers; they can wade halfway to the spot where the old ship-of-the-line lies fewer than 100 yards off shore, in only 20 feet of water.

Visibility is usually poor, and it worsens when sediment is disturbed by a diver's fins or by probing the bottom for the telltale green of oxidized fastenings. Diving near the end of a flood tide increases the chances of improved visibility for two reasons: Water from Block Island Sound is clearer than that from Peconic Bay, and with the water still moving, sediment raised by probing or fanning the bottom will be carried away, out of the diver's search area.

At a depth of 20 feet, only the amount of air carried determines the duration of a diver's stay on the bottom. While there, the throbbing engines of the Greenport–Shelter ferry interrupt on a regular schedule. It is difficult to ignore them, but after the initial distraction, they provide a background accompaniment for the dive. Small sailing craft pass silently overhead; for that reason, they are more dangerous to a surfacing diver than speeding outboards with their high-pitched engine whine warning of their presence. Divers must exercise extreme caution to avoid boat traffic when surfacing. There are two other recommendations for diving

Not much of Ohio *remains above the sand bottom. Even scattered planks and beams such as these are hard to find in the poor visibility. Photos by Mike Casalino.*

Ohio. The first is to observe the state law that divers must tow a float with a dive flag attached, and the second is to carry a compass to guide yourself back to shallow water, away from the dangers of the main boat channel.

Artifacts. Once divers have reached the wreck, the real work begins. Only painstaking, patient efforts reap rewards — a piece of sheathing, a fastening, or a bottle. The artifacts may be bronze, copper, iron, wood, or glass, but catch bags may also collect clams or an occasional lobster. Many copper and bronze fastenings have been found close to shore in only four to six feet of water.

The dive is not as challenging as some others, the wreck is far from picturesque, and the potential for artifacts is uncertain. Other, less tangible rewards attract amateur underwater historians; to them, the old hulk is a memorial — the forerunner of today's battleship. They know that the few scattered timbers and copper nails now exposed once sailed in glory as the pride of an emerging U.S. Navy, the grand old ship-of-the-line, U.S.S. *Ohio*.

H.M.S. *Culloden*

Approximate depth: 20'
Average visibility: 20'
Expertise required: Novice if no current
Current/surge: Slight to strong
Bottom: Sand and rocks
Location: Culloden Point, Montauk, NY

Launched: 1776
Sunk: January 24, 1781
Cause: Grounding during a storm
Type: British ship-of-the-line
Length/beam: 170'/47.1'
Tonnage: 1,658
Condition: Most of the remains are buried under the sand

History. April 17, 1746, marked the bloody Battle of Culloden — the critical conflict for the throne of England between the Royal army of the House of Hanover and the forces of Bonnie Prince Charles, claimant to

The British ship-of-the-line Culloden. *Courtesy of the Suffolk County Historical Society.*

the throne for the House of Stuart. That claim was forever silenced by the resounding defeat of Charles and his supporters on the Scottish moors of Culloden and Dunmossie.

The decisive victory so impressed the British that the following year a new warship was named for the battle site. That first H.M.S. *Culloden* sailed under the British flag for 27 years, until she went out of commission in 1770. Six years later, a new *Culloden* was launched at Deptford on May 18, 1776 — only seven weeks before the American colonies declared their independence. The warship, symbol of England's victory over the insurgents of Scotland, was destined to be lost in the American Revolution.

The new 74-gun ship-of-the-line carried 650 officers and ratings under Captain George Balfour, who remained in command for the life of the vessel. She spent her first year intercepting French or Spanish ships supplying the rebellious American colonists. Her first American encounter, the capture of a small Colonial merchant vessel bound for Bordeaux, occurred during the winter of 1777.

French sympathies for the American cause led to an open alliance between the two, and war between England and France. A French fleet of 16 warships sailed for America in April 1778. The British countered by sending a powerful fleet of 14 ships, including *Culloden*.

The Atlantic crossing was a disaster for the British fleet. It was battered by torrential storms and gale-force winds. Six ships were lost, and the eight that limped into Sandy Hook, NJ, needed major repairs before they were fit for action.

The French fleet was still to be dealt with, but it lay safely anchored in Boston harbor as the English left the protection of Sandy Hook to fulfill their mission. En route to Boston, a fierce Atlantic gale struck the northeast, and the British ships were again buffeted and battered by nature.

Culloden, only two years old, was dismasted and swept to sea, a target for total destruction if another Atlantic storm should strike. Fortunately the weather held, and she managed to limp home to England by December 1778 for refitting after six months of furious battle — against neither the French nor the Americans, but the forces of nature.

The French remained active in the American colonies, where they created a major problem for British interests by establishing a strong base at Newport, RI.

In September *Culloden* and several other British warships were ordered to New York as reinforcements. In October she participated in the capture of the 20-gun American privateer *Washington*.

Sinking. On January 20, 1781, the British received word that several French warships at Newport were about to run the British blockade. *Culloden, America,* and *Bedford* were ordered to intercept them if such an attempt was made. They rendezvoused in Block Island Sound on the 22nd. The next night, a heavy winter storm struck the area, packing the kind of violence the *Culloden* crew had good cause to remember. She was severely battered, as she had been three years earlier. Gale-force winds lashed the three ships with sleet and snow that blinded half-frozen lookouts.

The British ships headed for the open sea to ride out the storm. There could be no danger; every half hour, a crewman was taking soundings with a 20-fathoms hand lead without finding bottom.

At 4 a.m., the pilot was in the captain's cabin discussing the situation with Balfour. Without warning, pounding surf and coastline loomed directly ahead. When informed of the danger, Balfour raced on deck and ordered the anchors cut free to keep the vessel offshore. But before the crew could comply, *Culloden* shuddered violently; her copper-clad bottom had run fast aground. Shortly after, her rudder broke in two and was lost. The shore, barely visible through darkness and foul weather, led the pilot to conclude that the ship had grounded on Block Island. Dawn revealed that it was really Welles Point (known today as Culloden Point), near the northeastern edge of Fort Pond Bay, not far from Montauk Point, Long Island.

The warship could not be saved and Balfour ordered everything possible transferred to shore. Powder, gunner's stores, blocks, sails, carpenter's stores, pitch, and tar were stacked under tents for protection. Even water-soaked bread was laid out to dry.

The French ships that were reported to be running the blockade fared much better. They had returned to their protected harbor the day before the storm. By that action, they gained a total victory over the British who suffered a major defeat — by Mother Nature.

Blocks and tackle removed at least 46 cannon, gun carriages, and anchors from *Culloden*. The 28 obsolete 32-pound iron cannon, not worth salvaging, were spiked and toppled over the side, and the ravaged hull was set afire. Saddened British seamen watched their proud ship-of-the-line burn to the waterline in less than four hours.

Admiral Marriot Arbuthnot conducted a preliminary investigation of the *Culloden* disaster. His finding was that the pilot believed his ship had already cleared Montauk Point and could safely bear due south. On March 28, 1781, a court martial was held and the judge advocate merely reprimanded the pilot for using the wrong sounding lead; Admiralty regulations called for a heavier (50-lb) deep-sea sounding lead every half hour instead of the hand lead.

The Dive. The remains of *Culloden* lie almost entirely embedded in the sand shoal to the east of Culloden Point. When most of the wreckage is covered by sand, the wreck site can be recognized by small flint nodules lying in the sand. Five cannons, many cannon balls, and large pieces of wooden hull were exposed during the summer of 1991. Considerably more wreckage was exposed than had been in previous years. Visibility is best near the end of a flood tide. A strong current may be present when the tide is running.

Artifacts. After the British left the *Culloden* remains, Joseph Woodbridge of Groton, CT, salvaged 16 of her 32-pound iron cannon.

Another salvage attempt, headed by the caretaker of Gardiner's Island in 1796, removed iron fittings, copper bolts, sheathing, and the remaining rigging. In 1815, Captain Samuel Jeffers, of Sag Harbor, used a diving

A bottle recovered from Culloden *during Dr. Moeller's excavation of the site. Photo by the author.*

bell to retrieve 12 tons of pig iron and a 32-pound cannon. That was the last disturbance of the wreck for 158 years. During that time, Welles Point became known as Culloden Point. The location, mostly covered with underbrush, is now Culloden Shores, a development with only a few scattered homes. *Culloden* lives on in the identity of the historic site.

Carlton Davidson of East Moriches, NY, located the main part of the wreck, including its hull and five cannon, in 1973. He raised one cannon and donated it to the town of East Hampton. The cannon has been preserved and placed on display at the town's marine museum.

Carlton Davidson, on the right, and the Culloden *cannon he recovered. Courtesy of C. Davidson.*

Culloden *cannon on display in the East Hampton Town Marine Museum. Photo by the author.*

An East Hampton Town Marine Museum display of the wreck location during mapping, sketching, and excavation of the site by Dr. Moeller. Photo by the author.

Dr. Henry Moeller, New York Ocean Science Laboratory, was granted a permit to perform scientific study, map, photograph, and ultimately perform archaeological excavation of the *Culloden* site.

Dr. Moeller worked the site with students of his underwater archaeology class from the summer of 1976 through the summer of 1979. They airlifted part of the wreck, and recovered a multitude of artifacts — wood, leather, hemp, glass, pottery shards, cannon balls, a hand grenade, lead shot, pewter spoons, buckles, buttons, copper sheathing, nails, and barrel hoops. Their identification, classification, and preservation are a continuing program at the East Hampton Town Marine Museum.

From year to year, winter storms expose parts of the wreckage or artifacts, such as the cascabel of a sand-covered cannon, cannon balls, timbers, and planking. They may be observed and photographed, but not removed. The site has been placed under New York State protection, with severe restrictions against the unauthorized removal of artifacts.

Amsterdam

Approximate depth: 20'
Average visibility: 35'
Expertise required: Novice if there is no surge
Current/surge: Slight to extreme
Bottom: Sand and rocks
Location: About 3 miles west of Montauk Point on the south shore
Loran numbers: 43945.1 69859.9

Launched: 1866
Sunk: October 21, 1867
Cause: Fog
Type: Freighter
Length/beam: 211.4'/29.1'
Tonnage: 639
Condition: Flattened, scattered wreckage; the engine is exposed at low tide

History and sinking. Many ships have grounded on the treacherous reefs and shoals of Montauk Point, even in clear weather. When that projection of land is shrouded in fog, the navigational hazard is immeasurably worse. That was particularly true before the invention of radar and Loran.

In 1867 the iron-hulled British steamer *Amsterdam*, loaded with a cargo of fruit, wine, and lead, left Malaga, Spain, en route to New York. On October 21, while in a dense fog, she struck rocks about three miles west of Montauk Point, on the south shore. The freighter's hull was badly damaged and she was partially filled with water. Cargo, strewn along the beach for miles, was quickly gathered up by the locals. The cargo was insured for 6,000 pounds sterling by the Great Western Insurance Co. An agent of the company traveled to Montauk to oversee the salvage of what remained of the cargo. The freighter, less than a year old, and valued at 30,000 pounds, was declared a total loss. Only half of the cargo could be salvaged. None of *Amsterdam*'s crew survived. They were buried 1½ miles east of the lifesaving station.

The Dive. The wreck is only about 50 yards offshore but lies off property that is privately owned, so access is by boat only. Visibility depends on the strength of the surge, which determines the amount of sand suspended in the water.

The freighter's engine extends above water at low tide. The engine, covered with seaweed, is often mistaken for a rock, but closer inspection reveals the cylinder openings. Sections of iron hull are scattered about the bottom. From year to year the shifting sand either exposes or covers much of the wreckage.

Artifacts. In 1978 a marine biology student found a complete porthole lying in the sand about 50 yards south of the engine. The following year several deadeyes were recovered from a large piece of wreckage west of the engine. Any remaining artifacts are now buried under the sand.

Amsterdam's engine, exposed at low tide, allows the wreck to be located without Loran. Photo by the author.

The schooner John C. Fitzpatrick *before her conversion into a coal barge. Courtesy of the Dossin Great Lakes Museum, Detroit, MI.*

John C. Fitzpatrick

Approximate depth: 130'-135'
Average visibility: 35'
Expertise required: Advanced
Current/surge: Moderate
Bottom: Sand
Location: About 7½ miles south of East Hampton, NY
Loran numbers: 26135.6 43770.4(.8)

Launched: 1892
Sunk: April 3, 1903
Cause: Explosion
Type: Schooner barge
Length/beam: 242'/39'
Tonnage: 1,277
Condition: Scattered, low wreckage

History. The conversion of large sailing ships into coal barges became a common practice toward the end of the 19th century. The vessels were generally two-masted, after conversion, carrying fore and aft sails that provided too small a spread of canvas for such large ships, some of which drew as much as 20 feet of water. The sails were barely adequate for making headway under good conditions. In stormy seas, they were at a disadvantage.

The coal-carrying barges (usually two or more at a time) were towed from one port to another by a steamer or tug. That reduced transportation costs since the former sailing transports were no longer at the mercy of adverse winds, required no fuel, and were staffed by small, inexpensive crews. However, many barges were lost when tow lines parted in rough seas (see *Panther*). Such disasters were so frequent that in January 1895, four were wrecked in Long Island Sound, with 12 lives lost.

Research revealed that the graceful four-masted schooner *John C. Fitzpatrick* suffered the indignity of being converted into a coal barge, and was towed from port to port by a steam tug.

Sinking. On April 3, 1903, the *John C. Fitzpatrick* was en route from Philadelphia to New Bedford, MA, with 24,000 tons of coal. She was under tow by the tug *Sweepstakes*. The schooner barge had steam-powered equipment for hoisting the anchor and cargo. Off East Hampton, the boiler for the equipment exploded, blowing a large hole in the barge's wooden hull and sending her to the bottom.

The Dive. Divers should be aware that several washout areas around the collapsed and broken-up hull are approximately 135 feet deep. Wreckage extends only a couple of feet off the bottom. Divers seldom visit this wreck, but when they do, they quickly find that the scattered ribs and timbers are a haven for large lobsters.

Artifacts. The scattered wooden wreckage, located 7½ miles south of East Hampton, NY, had been referred to as the "Jug" since its discovery because trawlers had recovered a couple of ceramic jugs in their nets. Dick Ziminski, a member of the Aquarian Dive Club, recovered two 25-lb lobsters on the wreck on the same day in the mid-1970s. In 1988, Ron Barnes, another member of the Aquarians, finally identified the wreck with his recovery of a bronze capstan cover engraved "John C. Fitzpatrick, American Ship Windlass Co., Providence RI, 1892. F.W. Wheeler & Co. Shipbuilder, West Bay City, Michigan."

The schooner barge is considered to be an excellent lobster wreck, but not a good artifact dive.

Panther

Approximate depth: 55'	**Launched:** 1870
Average visibility: 30'	**Sunk:** August 24, 1893
Expertise required: Novice	**Cause:** Storm
Current/surge: None to moderate	**Type:** Tug
Bottom: Sand and silt	**Length/beam:** 191'/36'
Location: 1½ miles south of	**Tonnage:** 712
Southampton, NY	**Condition:** Scattered wreckage
Loran numbers: 26248.7 43802.0	

History and sinking. On August 21, 1893, the 186-foot, three-masted coal barge *Lykens Valley* left Philadelphia for Newburyport, MA, with a crew of four and a cargo of 2,350 tons of coal. She was under tow by the steam-driven, sail-rigged ocean tug *Panther*, with a crew of 16 and carrying 739 tons of coal. The iron-hulled tug was one of the largest of her kind afloat, one of 20 such ships owned by the Philadelphia and Reading Railroad Company.

The tug Panther *towing two schooner barges. Courtesy of the Suffolk County Historical Society.*

Three schooner barges prepare to leave harbor under tow. Courtesy of the Suffolk County Historical Society.

On the morning of August 24, six miles off Southampton, NY, a fierce storm that proved to be the edge of an offshore hurricane struck the two vessels. *Panther*'s captain, George W. Pierson, feared that, tied together, both vessels might be lost in the tempest. He ordered the barge cut loose, leaving it to drift helplessly onto a sandbar ½ mile east of St. Andrews Dune Church.

Inhabitants of a house near the beach watched helplessly as two of the barge's four-man crew were washed overboard by 20-foot breakers. All four were lost. The fury of the storm was so severe that the coal-laden barge broke up within an hour. An observer reported that, "There was nothing to see but wreckage chopped up by the force of the sea as to be hardly recognizable as that of a ship."

After cutting loose from *Lykens Valley*, Captain Pierson tried to save *Panther* by turning the tug into the storm and moving offshore. Struggling against tremendous seas, the tug's deckhouse was destroyed by mammoth waves. Seawater poured into the engine room and drowned the boilers, leaving the vessel as helpless as the barge she had abandoned.

The seas kept coming mountain-high, sweeping clear over the boat. Life preservers were issued and many of the crew climbed the rigging only to be swept into the sea by the huge waves. The top of the pilothouse had been torn loose, and one of the crew climbed on top of it as it drifted by. He floated on that wreckage for a long while until it turned over, his last recollection until he came to on shore.

Another member of the crew estimated that he had been in the water for about three hours before he felt land beneath his feet. He clawed into the sand to grasp the hand of one of the members of the rescue team that had formed a human chain extending off the beach. The rescuers, who also recovered two other survivors, were volunteers from the neighboring cottages working with the crew of the Southampton Life Saving Station.

The survivors lapsed into periods of unconsciousness as local physicians tended them. Their bodies were black and blue from the repeated pounding they had endured amidst the wreckage. They were physically and mentally exhausted by the ordeal of a close brush with death at sea.

Of the 20 men aboard the two vessels, only three of *Panther*'s crew survived. *Lykens Valley* lost all four of her crew even though the barge was close to shore when she broke up. For several weeks, bodies in various stages of decomposition washed onto southeastern Long Island beaches. All but one was recovered. Most were buried in the northwest section of the North Road Cemetery, with a memorial plaque marking the modest 10-by 20-foot plot.

When *Panther* sank she remained upright and pretty much intact except for the demolished deckhouse. Her heavy cargo of coal kept her in a fixed position. At low tide on a clear day, several feet of her mast was visible from shore. Lying in only 55 feet of water, she was considered a menace to navigation and on October 11, 1893, a nine-pound dynamite cartridge was lowered to the wreck from one of two surfboats from the local lifesaving station. The boats withdrew about 300 yards and electrically detonated the charge. A six-pound cartridge completed the task and the tug was effectively dismasted, as many timbers rose to the surface. Three days later, a headless body washed ashore near Bridgehampton. It was concluded that the last victim had been found, probably dislodged from the wreck by the explosions. The body was buried with the other victims of the disaster.

The Dive. *Panther*'s remains have been a favorite spot for fishermen for a century. The site has been visited by scuba divers since the late

Marker stone for 13 seamen in the old cemetery at Southampton. The barge's name is misspelled. Photo by Carlton Davidson.

1950s. Only a small amount of wreckage remains and it is scattered over the bottom. An iron screw-propeller and 30 feet of shaft leading to the engine extending about 14 feet off the bottom, part of a boiler, and a few metal plates are all that remain. There is not much wreckage to see, but the disappointment is amply compensated for by the large lobsters.

Artifacts. The 1,200-pound iron anchor of the barge *Lykens Valley* was discovered on September 28 between the offshore sandbar and the beach. Two boats with rope and tackle brought the anchor ashore. The anchor was purchased from the salvagers by the congregation of St. Andrews Dune Church. It was placed on the front lawn of the church as a memorial to the victims.

The church, built by the government as a lifesaving station in 1851, was ideally suited for such a memorial to men who lost their lives at sea. Within the church, one brass wall tablet records the wreck of *Panther* and *Lykens Valley*. Another memorializes the destruction of the British sloop-of-war *Sylph* on the night of January 16, 1815, with the loss of all but six of her 133 men. A cannon from the French ship *Alexandre*, which was wrecked in 1874, shares the front lawn of the church with *Lykens Valley*'s anchor.

Today a bronze valve or some other artifact may occasionally be found, but most divers find it more fruitful to search for lobsters. The flattened iron plates of *Panther* offer many niches for the tasty crustaceans.

Approximate depth: 15'
Average visibility: 25'
Expertise required: Novice to advanced, depending upon the surge
Current/surge: Slight to strong
Bottom: Sand Location: ½ mile east of Moriches Inlet
Loran numbers: 26420.5(.6) 43790.3(.5)

Launched: 1878
Sunk: February 8, 1900
Cause: Fog
Type: Passenger/freighter
Length/beam: 275'/38.5'
Tonnage: 1,997
Condition: The hull extends four or five feet above the sand

History. Inshore waters are constantly in motion. They respond to currents and changing tides with a restless action that carries sand from one place to another. That process results in a continuing cycle of beach erosion and buildup. As a consequence, many inshore shipwrecks are periodically exposed more at one time than another.

The passenger-cargo steamer *Gate City* is an outstanding example of such a wreck, and is at the mercy of the shifting sands of Long Island's south shore.

Gate City was built for the Ocean Steamship Company of New York in 1878. Stateroom accommodations were provided for 114 cabin passengers, and less luxurious accommodations for 30 steerage passengers.

The steamer could carry a cargo of miscellaneous freight in addition to passengers. Her main saloon was 80 feet long and 30 feet wide. It was finished in French walnut, bird's-eye maple, rosewood, and mahogany, all accented by elegant red plush upholstery.

The Boston and Savannah Steamship Company bought the vessel in September 1882 and placed her under the command of Captain Hedge. She was run between the two ports that made up the company's name, and she served in that role for almost four years. On July 16, 1886, *Gate City* left Savannah en route to Boston with 52 passengers and a full cargo that included a shipment of 53,000 watermelons. Three days later, dense fog drove in from the east as the vessel was entering Vineyard Sound. The engines were stopped while they waited for the fog to lift. After four hours, Captain Hedge felt that he could wait no longer and ordered slow speed ahead, with one of the seamen taking soundings to ensure against grounding. The seaman heaving the lead raised the alarm, "We have no water," at the instant the vessel ran aground off Naushon Island.

Passengers who recalled that only 30 months earlier *Gate City*'s sister ship, *City of Columbus*, had been lost only 11 miles away were shaken by the prospect of a repeat performance. Ninety-seven passengers and crew had been lost in that sinking at Devil's Bridge on January 18, 1884, the worst single marine disaster to occur off Martha's Vineyard.

Gate City had been moving cautiously through the heavy fog at the time of the accident and seemed to ground so lightly that it was felt she could be refloated without much of a problem. A salvage vessel carrying divers arrived at the scene on July 20. To lighten the steamer the watermelons were thrown overboard, transforming Vineyard Sound into a bobbing sea of green capsules. Many small craft harvested the unexpected crop; 10,000 of the melons floated ashore on Naushon Island and were then forwarded to Boston, their original destination.

The salvage company had little difficulty in refloating *Gate City*. They found the principal damage directly under the fire room, where a large boulder had forced through the plates. The opening was closed by sewing a dozen blankets together and wedging them into the hole. A huge canvas boot was placed under the bow to cover another large hole on the starboard side. On July 26, the vessel was pumped out and she was refloated. She steamed into Boston Harbor under her own power, accompanied by two tugs. The boot and blanket plugs had served their purpose.

Gate City resumed operations as soon as repairs were completed. She continued to operate for the next 14 years, with the exception of a brief enlistment as a troop transport in 1898. She carried 556 Spanish-American War soldiers from Cuba to Camp Wikoff, Montauk, NY, then returned to her familiar run.

A passenger from Gate City *is rescued by breeches buoy as others on the bow await their turn. Photo from the author's collection.*

Sinking. On February 8, 1900, *Gate City* was en route from Savannah to Boston under the command of Captain Goggins when she ran into a dense fog bank off Long Island. With the shoreline invisible, Goggins was unaware of his exact position. Perhaps because of faulty instruments or his own error in thinking the ship had cleared the Montauk Point tip of Long Island, Goggins headed directly into shore.

The vessel was under almost full steam when she drove hard onto the outer sandbar, three miles east of the Moriches Life Saving Station. Her whistle had been blowing for almost an hour while the steamer plowed through the fog at a speed that was probably too high for the limited visibility. The station's beach patrol had been monitoring the whistle, but the fog was too dense for their responding signals to reach the ship.

The sea was calm and the lifesaving crew launched a surfboat at once, guided to the stranded ship by her bell and whistle. Their offer to take off as many of the 49 passengers (including three women) and crew as their boat could carry was accepted only by the women. The others elected to stay because the steamship did not seem to be in any immediate danger.

The following day, the remaining passengers and 18 of the crew whose services were not required were taken off. It appeared that *Gate City* could be refloated without much problem; her hull was in good condition and she was facing toward the beach. A salvage steamer stood by and removed 2,713 bales of cotton and some barrels of turpentine. Then, a storm arose and worsened as the day progressed. That night the stranded steamer was driven over the sandbar that had been supporting her, into the section of shoaling beach, which is almost always fatal to a stricken ship.

The stranded steamer quickly became a tourist attraction. Photo from the author's collection.

Gate City *was heavily salvaged. Even iron hull plates, on the land side, were removed. Photo from the author's collection.*

Salvage of the cargo continued after the storm subsided. All of the cotton and much of the turpentine was recovered, but the ship was creeping closer to the beach with each tide. Several powerful tugs strained to pull the vessel from the sand into open water at each high tide for more than a week before the effort was abandoned. Instead of trying to save the ship, by that time valued at $100,000, efforts were redirected to dismantling and removing everything of value. Even huge iron hull plates were removed for sale as scrap.

A salvage tent camp, appropriately named "Sand Hill City," was set up on the beach, with one large tent serving as a hotel. The operation was so big that a rail line was constructed over Moriches Bay to the wreck site for transfer of the salvaged material. The magnitude of the large wreck and the massive recovery effort attracted hordes of spectators to the scene. The large ship was almost close enough to walk aboard from the beach at low tide. There were no roads on the barrier island, but hundreds arrived by boat to view the spectacle. The railway was dismantled when salvage ceased, and *Gate City* was soon forgotten.

In September 1938, a hurricane struck Long Island with such force that a new inlet was created at Moriches. That alteration in the shoreline affected tide and current action. Boatmen reported that a new wreck was exposed on the west side of the inlet, where none had been observed earlier. It was *Gate City*, rediscovered after 38 years of oblivion. It soon became a favorite fishing spot for large blackfish, attracted by the mussels that cover the wreck. Most of those who were interested in the wreck were unaware of its identity, only that it provided good fishing and was a potential menace to navigation.

The Dive. In the course of time, the inlet created at Moriches in 1938 migrated westerly along the beach until it was stabilized with jetties by the U.S. Corps of Engineers. The wreck is now about ½ mile east of the inlet and approximately 50 yards offshore. Scuba divers have explored the remains since the early 1960s. They never know from year to year how much of the wreck will be exposed above the shifting sands. Barrels of solidified turpentine in a cargo hold were partially in view in 1978; the next year they were deep in sand.

Gate City is a shallow dive of only about 20 feet. The surge may force a diver onto jagged or pointed scraps of metal. Several times I have been lifted from the ocean side of the wreck and dropped into the middle of the wreckage. These conditions are not ideal for photography. The turbulence is not only perilous; it destroys the visibility that is essential for photography.

Artifacts. Portholes, gauges, deadeyes, and many other artifacts were recovered following a savage winter storm that ripped a new inlet through the barrier island in January 1980, exposing *Gate City* more than at any time since sport divers first visited her.

Wrecks such as *Gate City* offer a continuing source of artifacts to patient divers, willing to wait for shifting sands to uncover hidden artifacts. She continues to present an ever-changing image to those who are interested in her existence, the preservation of her relics, and the adventure of underwater exploration.

Oregon

Approximate depth: 130'
Average visibility: 30'
Expertise required: Advanced
Current/surge: Slight to strong
Bottom: Sand
Location: 15 miles south-southwest of Moriches Inlet
Loran numbers: 26453.0(.2) 43676.2(.5)
Launched: 1883

Sunk: March 14, 1886
Cause: Collision
Type: Transatlantic passenger liner
Length/beam: 520'/54.1'
Tonnage: 7,375
Condition: A huge engine and nine large boilers in a massive pile of flattened wreckage. The bow is the most intact part of the wreck.

History. The traveling public has always been in a hurry to get from one place to another, whether in cars, trains, planes, or even luxury ships. It was to the public's fascination for speed that the steamship *Oregon* owed her existence. The course of the maritime race was monumental: the breadth of the Atlantic Ocean. The contestants were originally three British steamship lines: Cunard, Inman, and White Star. The prize was the Blue Riband (ribbon), a British maritime term for outstanding achievement. It was awarded for the fastest transatlantic passage, and served to inspire designers, builders, and owners to new levels of ocean liner speed.

Cunard took the record in 1863 with the steamship *Scotia*, which crossed the ocean at an average speed of 14 knots. Then the Inman Line took the award in 1867, and held it until the White Star Line established a new record of 16 knots in 1871 with *Britannic*. All the honors were British until Stephen Guion, president of the Guion Line, vowed to bring the Blue Riband to America.

In 1879, Guion launched *Arizona*, built by John Elder & Company of Govan, Scotland. To Guion's delight, *Arizona* averaged 17 knots on her maiden voyage and won the Blue Riband. He followed with the larger and more powerful *Alaska*, which made the crossing in under seven days at a speed of 17.76 knots.

Cunard responded by ordering two new superliners, *Eturia* and *Umbria*, from the builders of *Arizona* and *Alaska*. Guion struck back. In 1881, he directed the builders to lay the keel of *Oregon*. Two years later, she won the Blue Riband with a speed of 18 knots.

The new empress of the sea was constructed of iron. Her three-cylinder engine produced 13,575 horsepower. Each of her nine steel boilers were 16.7 feet long and 16.5 feet in diameter. Shipbuilders of the day shied away from reliance solely on steam power. Guion also included four full-rigged masts and sails.

The new liner was a "travelling palace," with 153 large, ventilated, and well-lighted staterooms, mostly on the main deck. Accommodations were provided for 340 first-class and 92 second-class passengers. Less commodious accommodations in the stern could handle 1,100 steerage passengers.

The loss of the passenger liner Oregon *was Cunard's first major disaster. Courtesy of The Mariners' Museum, Newport News, VA.*

In April 1884, Oregon *broke her own record for the fastest passage across the Atlantic.*
Mementoes such as this were probably given or sold to passengers. The passenger liner is
referred to on the memento as U.S.M.S.S. Oregon, *which stands for "United States Mail*
Steam Ship." When Guion sold her to Cunard, she became R.M.S. Oregon *Royal Mail Ship.*

The grand saloon was on the main deck, forward of the engines. Its
dimensions were 65 feet long by 54 feet wide, so lofty that the lowest
ceiling was 9 feet high. Parquet flooring underfoot and a white-and-gold
ceiling overhead were separated by walls adorned with satinwood panels
and gilded walnut pilasters. A massive cupola extended 20 feet above
the center of the ceiling.

Oregon flew the American flag for only 12 months. By June 1884,
Guion was in desperate financial condition. Boiler design problems and
the too rapid expansion of his fleet — three large liners in four years —
had depleted his resources. The shipbuilder, still waiting to be paid,
repossessed *Oregon* and sold her to the Cunard Line. It was a bitter blow
for Guion, particularly two months later when the new Cunard liner
recaptured the Blue Riband for the British with an average speed of 18.16
knots. A year later another Cunard liner, the giant *Umbria*, captured the
coveted award.

Oregon was the last American ship to hold the transatlantic record until
1952, when *United States*, which had a maximum speed of 38.32 knots,
established new Atlantic speed records.

Oregon had contributed only briefly to Cunard's long reign as the
fastest transportation between Europe and America. But she would be
long remembered for her role in the shipping line's first major disaster
in 43 years.

Sinking. In the predawn of Sunday, March 14, 1886, *Oregon* steamed
at full speed toward New York. Only 673 passengers and a crew of 205

were aboard. Despite those impressive numbers, it was less than half the vessel's capacity.

The time was about 4:20 a.m., and most of the passengers were still asleep. Captain Philip Cottier was below and First Officer William Matthew was on the bridge. The few passengers who were awake and on deck observed the lights of a vessel approaching on a northeast tack. None granted the approaching vessel more than passing attention until she suddenly loomed up on the port rail. The vessel was a heavily laden three-masted schooner that seemed oblivious to the luxury liner in her path. The schooner drove hard into the iron plates of *Oregon*'s port hull, amidships. The liner shuddered under the impact, but the wooden schooner rebounded and drifted off, seemingly out of control. The sea gushed in and flooded the liner's boiler room, stopping the engine. *Oregon* was left helpless, with her hull open to the sea.

Confused passengers milled aimlessly on the open decks, half-dressed or in pajamas and nightgowns. Steerage passengers were crying, screaming, and praying. Above the uproar could be heard the profanity of begrimed and half-dressed firemen and stokers. They seemed to have mutinied; officers had little or no control over them. Ladies and children were so roughly pushed about that several were thrown violently to the deck. The officers, assisted by some of the male cabin passengers, had to use belaying pins to subdue the mutinous men and prevent them from taking all the lifeboats. However, the first away was filled with them.

Rescue of Oregon's *passengers and crew. Courtesy of the New York Public Library.*

The lifeboats that were not commandeered by the firemen and stokers were filled with passengers in an orderly manner. But there were too few boats. Half the passengers, all male, and the crew were left behind with only life preservers, and would not survive for long in the cold water. It seemed that there was no hope for them.

Oregon was to have been guided through Ambrose Channel into New York Harbor by a pilot. That pilot was aboard the pilot boat *Phantom*, waiting to be placed aboard the liner, when *Oregon*'s distress signals were sighted. The pilot boat arrived at the scene at about 7 a.m., followed two hours later by a schooner.

By 11 a.m. all the passengers and crew were temporarily aboard the two small vessels. An hour later, the German steamship *Fulda* appeared and transferred the survivors aboard for transportation to New York.

At 12:45 p.m., approximately eight hours after the collision, *Oregon* went to the bottom. There was no loss of life on the liner, but the nine-man crew of the schooner, believed to be *Charles H. Morse*, went down with her.

Oregon was valued at $1,250,000 and her cargo of china, earthenware, fruit, fabrics, and sundries at $700,000. Other losses included $216,000 in personal effects of the passengers, and $1 million in negotiable coupons and currency. One female passenger claimed she lost $15,000 worth of diamonds.

A Court of Inquiry was held in England to determine the reason for the collision. The court found First Officer Matthews remiss in his calculation of distance between *Oregon* and the schooner, but not sufficiently remiss to warrant punishment. Cunard, however, held Captain Cottier responsible for the loss of *Oregon* and released him, even though he was not on the bridge at the time of collision. He was 45 years old, the youngest captain in the fleet, and had held his Master's papers for 20

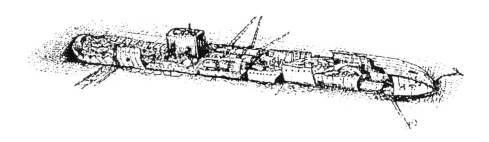

This sketch of Oregon *was made in 1979; the wreck has changed little since that time. The steamer's nine large boilers can be seen amidships in front of her massive engine. Courtesy of Steve Bielenda and Larry Listing.*

years in the employ of Cunard. His dismissal was justified by Cunard by his failure to check bulkhead doors daily, as specified by company policy. He had testified that with her large engine compartment bulkhead doors jammed open he could not save the ship.

No lives were lost in the *Oregon* disaster, but if there had been only two instead of eight hours between collision and sinking, many would have gone down with the ship. Fewer than half the passengers and crew could have been crowded onto the lifeboats and life rafts. Twenty-six years later, on April 14, 1912, *Titanic*, the largest passenger ship in the world, sank on her maiden voyage. More than 1,500 of 2,206 passengers and crew aboard perished because the maritime trade had ignored the warning given by the *Oregon*. A maximum of 1,178 people could have been accommodated by *Titanic*'s lifeboats, if they had been filled to capacity.

The Dive. More than 100 years after the steamship brought transatlantic speed honors to the U.S., she has become recognized as one of the most interesting and exciting dives on the northeast coast. Her depth varies from about 130 feet in the sand to approximately 120 feet on top of the rubble. A giant steam engine extends 60 feet from the bottom, and divers can cruise around the huge boilers. Two large blades of the iron screw-propeller thrust boldly out of the sand. When visibility is at its best, it

One of the first diver's to visit Oregon *rummages through scattered artifacts. Photo by Michael deCamp.*

All sport divers do not search for artifacts; many search for the large lobsters that are frequently found on the wrecks. Photo by Steve Bielenda.

seems to a diver descending the anchor line that the remains of the majestic luxury liner are rising to meet him at some halfway point.

However, the scattered wreckage can be disorienting to a diver, causing the diver to have difficulty in finding the anchor line upon completing the dive. A diver unfamiliar with the wreck should remain within sight of the anchor line or use a tether line.

The flattened hull plates are ideal habitats for lobsters.

Artifacts. The day after *Oregon*'s sinking, the Merritt-Chapman Wrecking Company dispatched hard-hat divers to the scene. *Oregon* was sitting upright with the tops of her masts out of the water.

Six divers worked through that spring and summer, removing mail and cargo while the ship gradually broke up. Most of the cargo was retrieved by the divers.

Today, portholes, bottles, silverware, and crystal decanters are occasionally recovered. Also, dinner plates, cups, and chamber pots bearing the Cunard Steamship Company or Guion Line emblems are among the varied artifacts still being found on the wreck.

Approximate depth: Exposed at low tide to 25'
Average visibility: 20'
Expertise required: Novice to advanced, depending upon the surge
Current/surge: Slight to extreme
Bottom: Sand
Location: About ½ mile west of Davis Park, Fire Island. The wreck is partially exposed at low tide.

Loran numbers: 26546.9(7.0) 43765.3(.4)
Launched: 1886
Sunk: March 25, 1893
Cause: Storm
Type: Tanker
Length/beam: 300'/37'
Tonnage: 2,307
Condition: Part of the steel hull and engine remain above the sand

History. The evolution of today's supertanker began when Colonel Edwin L. Drake struck oil near Titusville, PA, in 1859. That discovery led to a new branch of marine architecture, the construction or adaptation of ships to transport oil to Europe from the United States. Petroleum was originally transported in wooden kegs stowed in the holds of ships. *Glückauf* was the first steamer ever built expressly to transport oil across the Atlantic. Her design of large tanks built into the hull, with the engine room aft, has remained basically the same in today's tankers. She was built in England for the German-American Petroleum Company.

The tanker, a few inches more than 300 feet long and with a beam of 37 feet, was minuscule compared to the mammoth superliners that fol-

Glückauf was the first steamer ever built expressly to transport oil across the Atlantic. Courtesy of the Suffolk Marine Museum Collection, Sayville, NY.

43

lowed. Japan's tanker *Esso Atlantic*, launched in 1977, is one of the world's biggest ships. She is 1,334 feet long (more than the height of the Empire State Building) with a beam of 175 feet, and displaces 509,000 tons. Her paint alone weighs 400 tons, and her cargo capacity is 312,000 tons. *Glückauf* could carry only 2,600 tons of petroleum.

Glückauf was powered by a triple expansion engine, drawing steam from two boilers. The engine was aft, below a long poop deck. A small bridge amidships, a very long forward deck, and a short fo'c'sle completed the typical tanker silhouette. Sails were added to enhance her speed in fair weather and perhaps as insurance against breakdown of the steam propulsion system. The sails were later removed in favor of full dependence on the engines. The usual fore and aft centerline bulkheads were supplemented by transverse bulkheads, to create 16 storage tanks for petroleum.

The cargo tanks were separated from the coal bunkers and engine room by a cargo pump room that served as a cofferdam. A continuous fore and aft trunkway allowed for cargo expansion, with the lighter oils carried on each side. The vessel was lit throughout by electricity to minimize the danger of open-flame explosion.

Sinking. *Glückauf* arrived in New York on her maiden voyage on July 29, 1886, and operated successfully until 1893. En route to the U.S. on March 25, 1893, she went ashore on Fire Island, opposite Patchogue, NY. The tanker was under charter to the Standard Oil Company when, just before dusk, she was battered by a gale. Men from the Blue Point

This model of Glückauf *is on display at the National Museum of American History, Division of Transportation, Smithsonian Institution. Smithsonian Institution Photo No. 77-12439.*

Life Saving Station watched her being driven relentlessly toward the beach despite the drag of her anchors. She struck and stranded on the outer sandbar.

The lifesavers lit huge driftwood fires, and waited through the night for a chance to attempt a rescue. At daybreak, they set up a Lyle gun. The small brass cannon was loaded with a projectile to which a light but strong lifeline was attached. The line was carefully coiled inside a box beside the cannon to avoid tangles. The first shot sailed over *Glückauf*, amidships, and the line was quickly grasped by the tanker's crew. The shore end of the line was attached to a heavy cable and a breeches buoy that was dragged from shore to ship.

The cable was firmly attached to the ship, and her crew were brought to shore in pairs. The heavy cable sagged because of the long distance from shore. The rescued crew were dragged through rather than over the sea. The understanding team of lifesavers dispensed with the usual practice of hauling in the breeches buoy. In order to minimize the length of the rescued men's ordeal, they grasped the line and raced up the beach at top speed.

A salvage tug from New York braved the continuing gale for several days, and managed to attach hawsers to *Glückauf*'s stern, which lay seaward. They waited for an especially high tide before trying to free the tanker. On April 7, a very high tide coupled with another storm from the south loosened the stranded ship from the bottom, and the salvage tug

The German tanker ashore on Fire Island. Courtesy of the Steamship Historical Society Collection, University of Baltimore Library.

eased the tanker free. The storm increased in intensity as the tug began its tow. Then the hausers parted, and *Glückauf* was carried over the outer sandbar, onto the beach.

The steamer was stripped of most of her rigging, engine, and fittings and was then left for the sea to break up. She became a tourist attraction for the summer residents of Long Island's Great South Bay. Three years after she came ashore, *The New York Times* reported: "On a clear day she can easily be distinguished from the train on the Long Island Railway if you know where to look for her. On the ocean beach she is visible for ten miles either way, if there is not too much mist from the surf. Watching her from the bay, on the sail across from the mainland, it looks exactly as if she was trying to get across the Fire Island beach into the quiet waters of the Great South Bay."

The wreck remained in fair condition for many years. The more adventurous could climb aboard and wander all over her.

The Dive. Professional salvagers, souvenir hunters, vandals, the ocean, and time have taken their toll of *Glückauf*. In 1944, her boiler could still be reached on foot during extreme low tide. Parts of her are still exposed at low tide, but most of her remains are underwater. No one wanders about her now without snorkel or scuba equipment. A wreck symbol on nautical chart 12353 shows the location.

The wreck is about 75 feet offshore and the surge is a potential hazard. It could propel a diver onto jagged, metal wreckage. Visibility depends on the strength of the surge; the heavier it is, the more sand is suspended

Glückauf *is just offshore; a few pieces are exposed at low tide. Photo by the author.*

Exposed pipes within the remain's of the tanker's boiler. Photo by the author.

in the water, obscuring the vision of a diver who has come to see the first steamer built solely for the purpose of transporting oil.

Artifacts. The ocean and souvenir collectors took their toll of the wreck. Everything that man or the elements could carry away disappeared. Axes, saws, screwdrivers, wrenches, pry bars, and hatchets were used to hack, chew, and pry mementos from the wreck. When there was nothing to be found worth taking, idle hands were kept busy disfiguring the remains with initials, names, even product advertising.

Today scattered wreckage in the stern, located in about 25 feet of water, offers the best chance to find artifacts.

U.S.S. *San Diego*

Approximate depth: 110'
Average visibility: 30'
Expertise required: Advanced
Current/surge: Slight to strong
Bottom: Sand and silt
Location: 16 miles southeast of Fire Island Inlet
Loran numbers: 26543.3 43693.2

Launched: 1907
Sunk: July 19, 1918
Cause: German mine
Type: U.S. armored cruiser
Length/beam: 503.9'/69.5'
Tonnage: 15,335 fully loaded
Condition: Keel up; the hull is relatively intact

History. The keel of the armored cruiser *San Diego* was laid in 1902 at the Union Iron Works in San Francisco, CA. Five years later she was first commissioned U.S.S. *California.* Her designed complement was 47 officers and 782 enlisted men.

Guns bristle from the sides of California *at San Diego, CA, in 1910. Courtesy of the Naval Historical Center.*

The ship's impressive armament consisted of fifty guns; four 8-inch, fourteen 6-inch, eighteen 3-inch, twelve 3-pounder, two 1-pounder, four .30-caliber guns, and two submerged 18-inch torpedo tubes.

The principal wartime modification of *San Diego* was a reduction in her armament. The reason was twofold: to provide guns for auxiliaries and merchant ships, and to improve the watertightness of the warship for convoy duty under North Atlantic winter conditions. By 1918, several of the armored cruiser's 6- and 3-guns had been removed and the ports sealed.

Power was provided by two sets of four-cylinder, triple expansion, coal-fired engines driving twin screws, with a coal capacity of 2,685 tons. Five to six inches of tapered armor plate protected the hull against enemy fire, above and below the waterline. During her trials, the new armored cruiser produced 22.20 knots.

The armored cruiser served as *California* until Congress passed legislation reserving the names of states for battleships. On September 1, 1914, she was renamed *San Diego*. She was in constant demand for convoy service throughout World War I. Thousands of Allied seamen and troops, terrified by the threat of Germany's U-boats, were reassured by her impressive presence as their escort on hazardous transatlantic crossings.

Sinking. It is generally agreed that *San Diego* was sent to the bottom by a mine laid by *U-156*, one of Imperial Germany's underwater fleet assigned to maraud the eastern seaboard of the United States. For the first time since the War of 1812 more than a century earlier, a foreign power brought naval hostilities to the coast of America. (However, the German U-boat crew forever lost their opportunity to celebrate their coup

Engraving of U.S.S. San Diego *issued for the Panama-California Exposition, 1915. Courtesy of the Naval Historical Center.*

and answer how it was accomplished when *U-156* disappeared while returning to her home port. It is ironic that she was last reported trying to penetrate a massive mine field that the U.S. Navy had planted in the North Sea.)

On the morning of July 19, 1918, only four months before the Armistice that ended World War I, *San Diego* was under way to New York from Portsmouth, NH. At about 10 a.m., a lookout alerted Captain H.H. Christy to a small object moving on the surface. Its speed was faster than the prevailing current, leading to speculation that it might be a U-boat.

The threat of a U-boat galvanized *San Diego*'s gun crews into action. After several rounds were fired, the unidentified target disappeared, further supporting the belief that it was a U-boat. Lookouts became even more alert, yet less than an hour later, the zigzagging cruiser shuddered from an external explosion that shattered her portside hull, and from two massive internal blasts that erupted in the boiler room. Her gun crews again sprang into action, firing at every real or imagined object within range, but they were too late to avert disaster. The port engine was destroyed by the initial explosion. Full speed ahead on the starboard engine was ordered in an effort to beach the warship before she sank, which only hastened the inevitable, as tons of seawater, driven into the ruptured hull by the vessel's forward speed, drowned the remaining engine.

Armored cruiser California, *later renamed* San Diego. *Courtesy of the Naval Historical Center.*

San Diego wallowed at the mercy of the Atlantic as Captain Christy gave the order to abandon ship. Hundreds of seamen huddled in lifeboats, clung to rafts, or treaded water. They watched the big cruiser slowly capsize and disappear underwater within 30 minutes of the first blast.

Close proximity to shore, quick response by rescue vessels, and calm seas assured a high survival rate. Only six lives were lost: three by the initial explosion, one by a collapsing funnel, one by a falling lifeboat, and one when a lookout was trapped inside the cage mast.

U.S. Navy divers visited the wreck to determine the feasibility of salvage. They found *San Diego* bottom up, her keel at the bow only 36 feet under water. A commercial salvage company, contracted to conduct a more extensive survey, found that the bridgeworks had collapsed and the top of the turrets were touching the sand. In addition, thousands of rivets had shaken loose, opening seams in the hull. Even if the gaping hole in the engine room could be patched, the wreck could never be made watertight.

The wreck lay undisturbed for more than three decades, until the early 1950s, when a Freeport, NY, fisherman returning from Montauk observed a large profile on his depth recorder. Following up that chance observation, he noted the Loran numbers and returned the following day. He had rediscovered the lost warship, already a bountiful, artificial reef, ideal for fishing.

The Dive. The only major U.S. warship lost in World War I lies inverted, her superstructure buried in sand and her keel uppermost. She rests in this humiliating posture under approximately 110 feet of water, with a depth of about 65 feet to the upended keel.

The huge opening created by the German mine allows easy access to the engine room. The internal explosions that followed the initial blast left another gaping hole that provides easy entry into the boiler room.

50

The interior of *San Diego*, like any shipwreck immersed in seawater for six decades, is no longer recognizable as a ship. Some bulkheads and partitions have collapsed, and in some areas, decks have rusted through. Piles of debris and twisted wires, cables, and conduits are scattered about like an underwater junkyard. Layers of silt and sediment vary in depth from one inch to several feet throughout the wreck. When divers swim through such an interior, their fins stir up that loose material and cloud visibility. All familiar landmarks cease to exist.

Most experienced divers use a reel with several hundred feet of line, tying off the loose end where they enter the wreck. When the penetration is finished, the line is reeled in as they follow it back to the wreck's exterior. Five divers have lost their lives inside the wreck, running out of air before they could find their way out. Another diver became entangled in an ascent line and drowned. It is worth noting that those divers who lost their lives within *San Diego* did not use penetration lines.

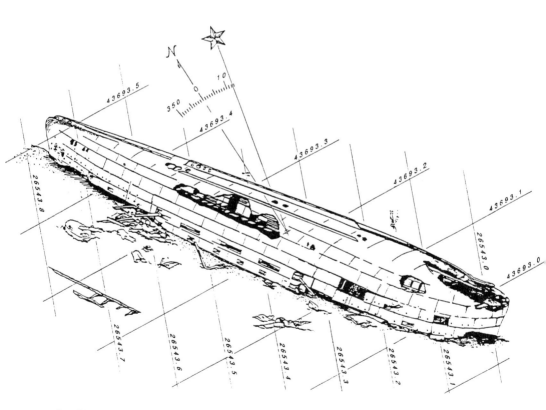

San Diego *lies inverted in about 110 feet of water. Many openings provide easy access for divers. However, penetration can be hazardous because of sediment and confusing passageways. Sketch redrawn by John Lachenmeyer from a drawing by Gary Gentile and K. Warehouse.*

Artifacts. The Navy sold salvage rights to Maxter Metals Company of New York City. Based on underwater photographs, the salvage operators planned to blow up the vessel's remains for its scrap metal value, at that time $70 a ton. Before the plan could be implemented, three concerned organizations, the American Littoral Society, the National Party Boat Owners Association, and the Association of Marine Angling Clubs, joined forces in opposition to this plan and founded the San Diego Fund. Their mutual objective was to preserve wrecks as marine habitats, and the destruction of any offshore wreck would defeat that purpose. Their effective lobby convinced the Navy to cancel the Maxter contract and adopt a policy that *San Diego* would remain undisturbed, never again to be offered for salvage.

The starboard screw-propeller was freed from its shaft with explosive charges by a group of unauthorized divers, but the Navy intervened, and the propeller was left lying on the bottom. While the authorities were monitoring the 37,000-pound bronze propeller, a group of six divers discovered that the port drive shaft had broken and the propeller was laying in the sand. They made off with it using a 200-foot tanker that had been converted into a salvage vessel. They rigged the propeller under the hull and started towing it toward Staten Island, NY. However, the propeller broke loose and was lost when it dropped to the bottom.

After the furor died down, a Long Island diver, operating under a salvage contract from a private group, attempted to raise the remaining propeller. The operation was set up with professional attention to detail, and a barge equipped with an A-frame to raise heavy objects. Equipment

A diver inspects the barrel of a 6-inch gun that is encrusted with marine life. Photo by Michael deCamp.

included underwater cutting gear, burning bars, a 600-cubic-foot-per-minute air compressor, 25 sets of doubles, 60 air storage bottles, and oxygen bottles.

The divers had lifted a large quantity of bronze from the wreck before they rigged the propeller for lifting. It was to be the last item of salvage. As the propeller was being raised, it fouled on a strut. Before the operator could declutch the crane motor, the A-frame was overstressed and its starboard leg was forced down four to five inches, opening a leak in the hull of the 700-ton barge, *Lehigh Valley 402*. Despite energetic pumping by the crew, water came in faster than they could pump it out. The 140-foot-long barge, a sizable wreck with a 45-foot beam and a large, 25'x20'x25' deckhouse, with all its expensive equipment, plummeted down to join *San Diego* on the bottom.

The barge, now broken up, still rests where she sank within 100 feet of *San Diego*'s starboard stern, a favored source of oversized lobsters for "bug-gathering" divers. The elusive propeller was eventually retrieved by others, who benefited from having had most of the labor performed for them.

Artifacts abound on the cruiser, but because it is a relatively easy dive with so many attractions to divert the unwary, care and common sense must be exercised. Winter storms and the corrosive action of the sea continue to open new sections of the wreck, providing access to additional areas of the ship's interior each year. She offers a constantly changing

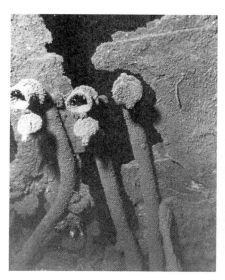

Speaking tubes for communicating between gun crews and the ship's magazines. They are inverted because of the upended position of the wreck. Photo by Jon Hulburt.

Scattered powder canisters for the 6-inch guns in one of the warship's magazines. Photo by Brad Sheard.

One of the engine room telegraphs. Recovered by and photo courtesy of Michael deCamp.

Divers from the charter boat Wahoo *were able to enter one of* San Diego's *storerooms in 1987. Lanterns, bugles, silverware, dinnerware, and other artifacts were recovered. The divers displaying their find on the dock are left to right: Sharon Kissling, Captain Steve Bielenda, Richie Kohler, Ed Murphy, John Lachenmeyer, Dan Berg, Don Schnell, and Richie Gomberg behind the rail. Photo by the author.*

cornucopia of souvenirs for sport divers, and her easy access, close to the shore of Long Island, has made her one of the region's most popular charter boat dive sites.

Many divers enter the ship's magazines to retrieve ordnance. Many find oak cylinders trimmed with copper and brass, powder canisters for the 6-inch cannon. Those canisters contain raw silk bags of compressed gun powder pellets. Vast quantities of other live ammunition have also been removed — to adorn walls, mantles, and tables in the homes of divers, friends, or relatives.

In June 1982 the Suffolk County Police bomb squad confiscated a 98-pound piece of ordnance that had been retrieved by a sport diver. The projectile for a 6-inch gun, contained 55 pounds of explosive. The object was too large to be handled at the Westhampton Beach Police bomb site and was transferred to the Army Ordnance Division for detonation at Fort Dix, NJ.

The Navy reacted to the incident through Lt. Joseph Tenaglia of the Naval Explosive Ordnance Disposal Team from the Earle Naval Ammunition Depot, NJ. A cadre of U.S. Navy personnel have received highly specialized training in dealing with unexploded ordnance. Lt. Tenaglia and a team of Navy divers toured several of *San Diego*'s magazines, guided by Steve Bielenda, noted Long Island scuba diver, and myself. The Navy concluded that the ordnance rooms should be sealed against further removal of live ammunition to prevent divers from endangering themselves. That action has not been taken; it probably never will be.

Armored cruiser *San Diego* lies dormant — but dangerous. She invites examination by the curious, and assesses a terrible penalty on the foolhardy or careless.

Hylton Castle

Approximate depth: 95'
Average visibility: 30'
Expertise required: Advanced
Current/surge: Slight to moderate
Bottom: Sand and silt
Location: 13 miles southeast of Fire Island Inlet
Loran numbers: 26569.4 43695.1(.3)

Launched: 1871
Sunk: January 11, 1886
Cause: Foundered
Type: Freighter
Length/beam: 251'/32.4'
Tonnage: 1,258
Condition: Scattered, low wreckage

History and sinking. The three-masted, iron-hulled British freighter *Hylton Castle* was overloaded with a cargo of grain when she foundered in a storm of snow, sleet, and rain, accompanied by hurricane force winds. There was no loss of life. The 15-year-old steamer was en route from New York to England when she sank on January 11, 1886.

After sinking, seawater soaked the grain cargo. As the grain expanded, it tore the hull apart.

The Dive. Steel plating is flattened and scattered over a large area, and partially buried in the sand. The most recognizable parts of the scattered wreckage are the boiler, engine, a winch, and an iron screw-propeller.

The wreck is usually a good dive for finding lobsters, as well as for spearfishing for sea bass and blackfish.

Artifacts. One small porthole is the only artifact Captain Steve Bielenda of the charter boat *Wahoo* recalls being recovered from the freighter.

Kenosha

Approximate depth: 105'
Average visibility: 25'
Expertise required: Advanced
Current/surge: Slight to moderate
Bottom: Sand
Location: 14 miles south southeast of Fire Island Inlet
Loran numbers: 26598.9(9.0) 43644.7(.8)(5.1)

Launched: 1894
Sunk: July 24, 1909
Cause: Foundered
Type: Collier
Length/beam: 243.7'/37'
Tonnage: 1,677
Condition: Two large pieces of flattened wreckage, a boiler, and a four-bladed screw-propeller

The collier Madagascar's name was later changed to Kenosha. *Courtesy of the Dossin Great Lakes Museum, Detroit, MI.*

The wooden-hulled wreck was mistakenly referred to as Fire Island Lightship, *even though the lightship had an iron hull. Courtesy of George Quirk.*

History and sinking. For many years a wooden-hulled wreck southeast of Fire Island Inlet was erroneously referred to as the "Fire Island Lightship." In 1986 Marc Weiss, an experienced wreck diver, diving with Steve Bielenda, captain of the dive charter boat *Wahoo*, recovered a brass capstan cover with the inscription "*Madagascar*, 1894, James Davidson, Ship Builder." Research revealed that the wooden-hulled *Madagascar* was built in 1894 in West Bay City, MI; 13 years later her name was changed to *Kenosha*. On July 24, 1909, the collier, a bulk-ore carrying vessel, foundered off Fire Island, without loss of life.

The *Fire Island Lightship* was a steel-hulled ship and the improperly identified wreck of *Kenosha* has a wooden hull.

The Dive. The wooden hull has flattened out, rising only a few feet above the sand. The large boiler and the steel four-bladed screw-propeller, still attached to its shaft, are easily recognized.

Large ribs and planks offer an excellent habitat for crustaceans, a bonanza for divers who find oversized lobsters. It is also an excellent wreck for spearfishing.

Artifacts. *Kenosha* is not a good artifact wreck.

Approximate depth: 20'
Average visibility: 20'
Expertise required: Novice if there is no surge
Current/surge: Slight to extreme
Bottom: Sand
Location: ¾ mile east of Fire Island Inlet

Loran numbers: 26674.0.(1) 43754.0(3)
Launched: 1895
Sunk: December 25, 1904
Cause: Ran aground
Type: Freighter
Length/beam: 340'/44.7'
Tonnage: 3,625
Condition: Scattered wreckage

History and sinking. Many ships en route to New York Harbor have grounded on Fire Island, but the first outward-bound vessel to run ashore there was the steamer *Drumelzier*. She was steaming for England and France when she grounded on Christmas Day 1904.

The freighter was not scheduled to leave Brooklyn until December 26, and the crew was anticipating Christmas ashore. Captain William Nicholson had other plans for his crew. Concerned that they might celebrate the holiday with too much enthusiasm and miss the scheduled departure time, on Christmas Eve Nicholson issued orders that all must remain

(continued on page 67)

The British freighter Drumelzier *aground on Fire Island. Courtesy of the Suffolk Marine Museum Collection, Sayville, NY.*

Two Culloden *cannon photographed by the author in 1988. The one with less deterioration was covered by sand.*

Wood timbers of the ship-of-the-line H.M.S. Culloden *are covered and uncovered by the shifting sand. Note the piece of copper sheathing, with a sheathing nail protruding, in front of the timbers. Photo by the author.*

The passenger liner Oregon*'s helm was found in October 1969, but was dropped and lost during the salvage attempt, and was never recovered. Photo by Michael deCamp.*

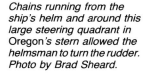

Chains running from the ship's helm and around this large steering quadrant in Oregon*'s stern allowed the helmsman to turn the rudder. Photo by Brad Sheard.*

Artifacts recovered from Oregon *by the author: bottles, Cunard chamber pot, Cunard dinner plate, and gifts found in passengers' luggage. The green bud vase is 8 inches tall. Photos by Aaron Hirsch.*

These artifacts recovered from Oregon *by Evelyn Dudas are inscribed or embossed with the Guion Line insignia. Photo by the author.*

This Oregon *bud vase, 6 inches tall, was recovered and photograped by Aaron Hirsch.*

Inside the passenger freighter Gate City's bow, showing deck supports. Photo by the author.

Two Gate City deadeyes. The steel cable leads to one that is partially covered with sand. Photo by the author.

Mike Casalino inspects wooden barrels of solidified turpentine in one of Gate City's cargo holds. Photo by the author.

The author with a porthole from Gate City. Photo by Carole Keatts.

Armored cruiser California, *later renamed* San Diego. *Courtesy of Bill Davis.*

George Quirk discovered storage compartments within San Diego's *bow. Quirk, in the center, and Joanne Doherty hold telescopes they recovered from one of the compartments. Courtesy of George Quirk.*

Lanterns George Quirk recovered from one of the compartments. Photos by Pete Nawrocky.

The barrel of a 3-inch gun projects out of San Diego's *hull, just above the sand. Photo by Brad Sheard.*

Cases of ammunition for the 3-inch guns inside one of San Diego's *many magazines. Photo by Jon Hulburt.*

Eight-inch projectiles inside one of San Diego's *magazines. Photo by Jon Hulburt.*

Springfield rifles inside the cruiser's armory. Photo by Jon Hulburt.

A case of ammunition (and a shell lying in the sand) for U.S.S. Tarantula's *deck gun. Photos by Pete Nawrocky.*

Ordnance recovered by the Aquarian Dive Club. Photo by Val Ackins.

The French freighter Iberia's *bow is one of the few recognizable parts of the wreck. Photo by Pete Nawrocky.*

Porthole, helm, bell, telegraph, and other artifacts recovered from the revenue cutter Mohawk. The bell bears the ship's name and year of launching. Photo by Val Ackins.

China recovered from Mohawk is embossed with the revenue cutter service insignia. Courtesy of Pete Nawrocky and George Quirk.

One set of the passenger liner Black Warrior's iron paddle-wheel hubs. Photo by Joe Bereswill.

Al Golden swims over Black Warrior wreckage. A ship fastening protrudes out of a wood timber in the foreground. Photo by Joe Bereswill.

65

Joe Gallo shines his dive light on a piece of the wreck referred to as "Seawolf." Photo by the author.

Joe Gallo inspects the wreck known as "Seawolf." Note the snagged fish net in the background. Photo by the author.

Jackie Nawrocky is framed by the remains of one of Mistletoe's *paddle wheels. Photo by Pete Nawrocky.*

Jackie Nawrocky looks through a porthole on the wreck known as the "G & D." Photo by Pete Nawrocky.

(continued from page 58)

aboard; none were to leave the ship. He decided to sail on Christmas morning to stop the grumbled complaints.

Drumelzier left the dock at 9 a.m. in a blinding snowstorm and very low visibility. Eight hours later she grounded on a sandbar off Fire Island. For some reason, Captain Nicholson or a member of his crew had managed to navigate an almost circular course. By that time the freighter, steaming at 12 knots, should have been well off Fire Island. Although the entire crew survived, the events aboard the freighter that Christmas Day have never been revealed. One possibility is that steel rails in the cargo caused a compass deviation. There are also suspicions that an unruly crew, overindulging in holiday spirits, was irresponsible or vindictive.

Only a moderate sea was running when the freighter grounded, but the wind swung it parallel to the beach, exposing it to heavy buffeting by the waves. Rockets and other distress signals went unnoticed by nearby lifesaving stations in the raging gale. The steamer was sighted the next morning, but her situation did not appear perilous.

Lifesavers offered to remove Captain Nicholson and his crew in surfboats, but Nicholson declined. He did allow 15 men from the Merritt-Chapman Wrecking Company to board his vessel to assist two salvage tugs trying to refloat the freighter. By afternoon the surf picked up, making conditions too rough for the lifesaving crews to launch surfboats, and the freighter was too far offshore to use a breeches buoy.

The seas increased and the salvage tugs were forced to move to deeper water, leaving those aboard *Drumelzier* on their own. Nicholson continued to insist that his ship was lying easy and that he wanted no assistance.

For the next two days the waves continued to build until heavy seas swept over the freighter's deck and part of the superstructure. The stranded steamship shuddered as the breakers pounded her against the sandbar. The men retreated below deck, while waves thundered against the steel hull. Rivets, forced out of hull plates, literally shot from starboard to port like bullets. A cannonlike report from deep within the hull was followed by a violent upheaval of the deck amidships. It was as if a volcanic eruption had occurred in her holds.

On New Year's Eve, with the temperature a brisk 18 degrees, 17 men were removed from the ship while ten-foot waves were still running. Nicholson and 13 others remained aboard in the numbing cold, without heat. They endured the discomfort while they waited for the salvage crew to begin removing the ship's cargo. Nicholson knew his ship was doomed because the hull was cracked and water lay several feet deep in the engine room. The boilers and engine had shifted six feet forward, and the keel had flattened. As the keel settled, the ship's funnel was projected three feet higher than normal above the deck. Nicholson and his skeleton crew remained aboard through all the travail to ensure that their ship would not be considered abandoned. That was significant in how much the salvage company would charge Astrat Shipping Company, Ltd., of Liverpool England, the freighter's owner.

Another violent storm followed; waves attacked the helpless ship with even more fury. Nicholson realized the perilous position he and his men were in. During a lull, he agreed to abandon the vessel. Subsequent salvage efforts recovered about 80 percent of the freighter's cargo of copper, steel, and lead, valued at $544,000.

The Dive. *Drumelzier*, built by J. Laing in Sunderland, England, was only nine years old when she came to grief on the sandbar near Fire Island Inlet.

The vessel is broken up, but her rudder quadrant is exposed at low tide. That accounts for fishermen referring to her as the "Quadrant Wreck." They frequently tie up to the exposed quadrant, which is still attached to a small piece of wreckage.

Two large boilers are situated about 150 feet east. The bow is another 150 feet further east. Between the two, hull plates, pipes, and other debris are scattered in the shifting sands that frequently cover, then expose, scattered pieces of the wreck.

Novice wreck divers can explore the remains of the old freighter, but only if there is no surge. Diving conditions must be checked first because the current and surge range from none to extreme.

Artifacts. *Drumelzier* is not a good artifact wreck, but is excellent for spearfishing.

U.S.S. *Tarantula*

Approximate depth: 115'
Average visibility: 35'
Expertise required: Advanced
Current/surge: Slight to extreme
Bottom: Sand
Location: 18 miles south of
Fire Island Inlet
Loran numbers: 26608.9 43609.6

Launched: 1912
Sunk: October 28, 1918
Cause: Collision
Type: Patrol vessel
Length/beam: 129'/19'
Tonnage: 160
Condition: Scattered, low
wreckage; bow still recognizable

History. "Live aboard a luxury yacht while you serve your country in the U.S. Navy." That prospect would swamp recruitment offices with volunteers willing and anxious to trade a few years of civilian life for duty to their country. But veterans of the service will attest that life aboard a U.S. Navy warship was never meant to be a luxury cruise. That explains why U.S.S. *Tarantula*'s crew was denied the privileges enjoyed by the rich and famous occupants of the vessel when she was a privately owned luxury yacht.

Tarantula *when she was a private yacht, above, and U.S.S.* Tarantula *after conversion into an antisubmarine patrol vessel, below. Courtesy of Bill deMarigny.*

W.K. Vanderbilt of New York ordered a motor yacht to be built at Newponset, MA. *Tarantula* was completed in 1912, but Vanderbilt would be able to use the luxuriously appointed yacht for only five years.

The U-boat threat, in both world wars, forced the U.S. Navy to acquire a small number of America's power-driven pleasure craft and convert them into antisubmarine patrol vessels. On April 25, 1917, the Navy acquired Vanderbilt's motor yacht and armed her with two 6-pounders and two 30-caliber machine guns. Designated SP-*124*, she patrolled the coastal waters of Connecticut, New York, and New Jersey for six months.

Sinking. On October 28, 1918, *Tarantula* was rammed by the Royal Holland Lloyd Line steamship *Frisia*. The subchaser quickly sank in about 115 feet of water.

In 1985 the wreck was identified when Bill deMarigny recovered the warship's bell. Photo by the author.

The Dive. For many years the wreck was referred to as the "Good Gun Boat Wreck" because of her armament. The deck guns, if still there, are buried in the sand, but ammunition for them and clips of rifle ammunition are scattered in the starboard bow area. In 1985 the wreck was identified when Bill deMarigny recovered the warship's brass bell with the ship's name inscribed on it. An occasional large lobster can be found.

Artifacts. Projectiles and brass shell casings for the deck guns, clips of rifle ammunition, and dinner plates are frequently recovered by divers.

Roda

Approximate depth: 25'
Average visibility: 20'
Expertise required: Novice
 if there is no surge and
 visibility is good
Current/surge: Slight to extreme
Bottom: Sand
Location: ½ mile off Tobay
 Pavilion, Tobay Beach,
 Fire Island

Loran numbers: 26741.3 43756.7
Launched: 1897
Sunk: February 13, 1908
Cause: Ran aground
Type: Freighter
Length/beam: 315'/44'
Tonnage: 2,516
Condition: Scattered wreckage

History and sinking. The British freighter *Roda* left Huelva, Spain, for New York on January 25, 1908, her hull loaded with copper ore. The steamer had been built in Dumbarton, Scotland, eleven years earlier; since then she had made many trips across the Atlantic. On February 13, the steel-hulled steamer grounded in a heavy fog on a sandbar off what is known today as Tobay Beach, Fire Island. The crew abandoned ship, but the officers remained on board as salvage tugs attempted to pull the steamer free. After two days, all hope of freeing the ship was abandoned, and so was the ship.

A winter storm broke the freighter's back, splitting the ship in half. Tons of copper ore, valued at $22,680, cascaded into the sea on either side of the sandbar. Another storm drove the lightened steamer closer to shore. The following summer, many local residents and summer visitors sailed across the bay to Fire Island to view the wreck. At low tide, the curious could wade out and climb a rope ladder to the freighter's deck.

The Dive. The beach has eroded over the years to the point where *Roda* is now approximately ½ mile offshore. The wreck is about midway between Fire Island Inlet and Jones Inlet. Visibility averages 20 feet, but it is subject to reduction by the current and surge.

The wreck, which has broken up, is partially exposed at low tide. Its bow, stern, stem, and a few other pieces that extend to within a foot of the surface are a potential hazard to boats and divers. The swirls of water denote submerged structure a foot or two beneath the surface. Frank Keating, a hunting and fishing columnist for the *Long Island Press* wrote on July 28, 1975: "*Roda* is a death trap for boats. . . . *Roda* has sunk or damaged more small craft than all other Island wrecks combined. Never a season goes by without some hapless boatman hanging his boat on a jutting spike. . . . Fishing the *Roda* is like playing Russian roulette."

This is a good wreck for novice wreck divers, but only if conditions are favorable — no surge and good visibility.

On this postcard, the British freighter Roda *is shown aground on Fire Island. Courtesy of the Suffolk Marine Museum Collection, Sayville, NY.*

Artifacts. Three years after the steamer stranded, the salvage tug *Howard*, with a crew of nine, attempted to recover the copper ore. She dropped anchor outside the outer sandbar, waiting for daylight before commencing operations. During the night, a summer squall blew the salvagers onto the bar; lifesavers rescued the crew before the salvage vessel broke up. The tug, also known as the "Scow Wreck," is in 25 feet of water. No further salvage attempts were launched.

Steel hull plates and other debris lie scattered about the bottom. *Roda* is not a good site for artifacts, but it is excellent for spearfishing.

Edwin Duke & Stone Barge

Approximate depth: 55'
Average visibility: 55'
Expertise required: Novice
Current/surge: Slight to moderate
Bottom: Sand and silt
Location: *Edwin Duke* lies 2 miles southeast of Jones Inlet. Stone barge lies 3 miles southeast of Jones Inlet.
Loran numbers: *Edwin Duke* — 26781.5 43737.0 (.1)

Stone barge — 26782.1(.5) 43728.2(.3)
Launched: Unknown
Sunk: Approximately 1930
Cause: Storm
Type: Tug and barge
Length/beam: Unknown
Tonnage: Unknown
Condition: The tug's slowly collapsing hull is recognizable; a pile of stones is all that is left of the barge

The tug Edwin Duke *was lost while towing a barge filled with jetty stones. Courtesy of Frank Persico.*

History and sinking. Sometime around 1930, according to Captain Frank Persico of the dive charter boat *Sea Hawk*, the tug *Edwin Duke* was towing a barge loaded with stones. The stones were to be part of the Jones Beach jetties, but both the tug and the barge foundered in a storm.

The Dive. The tug, lying on her starboard side in about 55 feet of water, is approximately one mile northeast of the barge she was towing. The pilothouse was ripped off by a trawler's net, and the hull is collapsing. The "Stone Barge," as the site is now known, is approximately three miles southeast of Jones Inlet, also in about 55 feet of water. Most of the wooden hull has disintegrated, but the many crevices among the pile of stones are ideal niches for lobsters. The wreck is also a good site for spearfishing.

Artifacts. Large portholes were recovered from the tug's pilothouse, and Captain Persico recovered several brass gauges. Today the wrecks produce very few artifacts.

Acara

Approximate depth: 25'
Average visibility: 15'
Expertise required: Novice if there is no surge
Current/surge: Moderate to extreme
Bottom: Sand
Location: Just east of Jones Inlet, about 500 yards offshore

Loran numbers: 26801.4(2.2) 43750.2(.8)
Launched: 1898
Sunk: March 1, 1902
Cause: Ran aground
Type: Freighter
Length/beam: 380'/47.3'
Tonnage: 4,193
Condition: Scattered, low wreckage, mostly under the sand

History and sinking. The steel-hulled British freighter *Acara* was en route from the Orient to New York when she grounded off Jones Beach on March 1, 1902. She had been built by Palmers Company, Ltd., in Newcastle, England, in 1898. The freighter had picked up cargo at Singapore, Shanghai, Foochow, and Hong Kong. Her holds were loaded with rubber, tin ingots, spices, indigo dye, tea, tropical plants, exotic birds, and an assortment of Oriental curios.

The freighter battled strong winds from the southwest in low visibility caused by heavy haze. Navigating blindly by dead reckoning, the captain miscalculated his position and ran the ship onto a sandbar. *Acara* had missed the entrance to New York Harbor by 25 miles. Towering waves crashed into the grounded freighter, kicking spray higher than her funnel.

The captain ordered full speed astern; the ship's screw-propeller churned up white foam, but failed to budge her from the sand.

The crew abandoned ship in two lifeboats; local historians described the survivors as "fierce-looking seamen." They were from India, Malaya, and China, wearing their respective countries' traditional clothing of turbans, scarfs, etc. The turbulent surf capsized one overloaded lifeboat, but without loss of life.

Salvage tugs arrived as waves drove *Acara* higher out of the water; she slowly spun about on a pivot point beneath her hull. Rivets holding steel hull plates together popped from the strain, and the hull broke in two, leaving the bow and stern to settle to the bottom separately.

The Dive. The wreck site, conveniently located near Jones Inlet, became a popular fishing site, and later a frequently visited dive spot. The remains of *Acara* are broken up and partially covered by sand. Some sections extend ten to 15 feet above the bottom.

If there is no surge, this dive is suitable for novice wreck divers. However, inshore wrecks such as *Acara* can be very dangerous with heavy surge. Under such conditions, it is hazardous for inexperienced divers.

Artifacts. Merritt-Chapman Wrecking Company was contracted to salvage the ship's cargo. Divers recovered 11,911 100-pound tin ingots. One manifest that the captain had brought ashore indicated that 14,800 ingots had been loaded aboard. Another listed 11,953. That means that after the completion of salvage, either 42 or 2,805 ingots were left in the freighter's holds. Of 50,000 cases of tea, 30,000 were salvaged. The amount of tea recovered by local residents led them to dub *Acara* "Our Tea Wreck."

The British steamer Acara *broke in two after stranding on Fire Island. Courtesy of the Suffolk Marine Museum Collection, Sayville, NY.*

Al Bohem with the two-blade section of screw-propeller he salvaged from Acara. Note that another diver has sawed the tip off one of the blades. Courtesy of Steve Bielenda.

Divers became interested almost immediately in salvaging the ship's screw-propeller. Its hub was of iron, but the blades were bronze. One diver sawed off the tip of a blade; others used a ten-foot extension pipe in a futile effort to unthread the iron nuts holding blade flanges to the hub.

During the winter of 1962-63, Robert Rickard, a pilot for Pan Am and an avid scuba diver, worked alone with a cutting torch to salvage the bronze blades. He devoted 25 days to the task over a period of several months. After cutting around each blade, he broke one loose with a steel cable hauled by his boat, then raised the prize with a lift bag and towed it to shore. When he returned several days later, he was dismayed to find that a two-blade section he had worked hard to cut around had been removed by two local divers, Al Bohem and Steve Bielenda.

Varied artifacts are still recovered at the *Acara* wreck site, including pieces of wooden tea crates, which is one reason the freighter is still referred to as the "Tea Wreck."

Lizzie D

Approximate depth: 80'
Average visibility: 15'
Expertise required: Intermediate
Current/surge: Slight to moderate
Bottom: Silt and sand
Location: 7 miles southwest of Jones Inlet
Loran numbers: 26828.8(9.0) 43696.3(.5)

Launched: 1907
Sunk: October 1922
Cause: Unknown
Type: Tugboat, rumrunner
Length/beam: 77.8'/21'
Tonnage: 122
Condition: No superstructure, but hull relatively intact

History and sinking.

Oh, we don't give a damn for our old Uncle Sam
Way-o, whiskey and gin!
Lend us a hand when we stand in to land
Just give us time to run the rum in.
> — *"The Smugglers' Chantey"*
> Joseph Chase Allen, 1921

Mystery surrounded the sinking of the rumrunner *Lizzie D* during the days of Prohibition. That mystery is still unsolved. The steel-hulled tugboat steamed out of Brooklyn on October 19, 1922, with a crew of eight, supposedly on a cruise of the narrows. Neither her crew nor the 15-year-old tugboat would be seen again for more than half a century. Prohibition was almost three years old and bootleg booze was big business. The Atlantic Ocean south of Long Island was known as "Rum Row," where hooch-laden ships from Canada would anchor just beyond U.S. territorial waters. Under cover of darkness, small vessels from American ports would transfer the illegal cargo and run it into some secluded shore. Many considered rum-running an almost respectable form of protest against the unpopular Eighteenth Amendment.

The U.S. Coast Guard attempted to enforce the antismuggling laws by adding more than 300 additional patrol boats and 25 former Navy destroyers. Many vessels were sunk during the unique 13-year "war" between rumrunners and the Coast Guard. What happened to the *Lizzie D* is still an unsolved puzzle. The tugboat had taken on a cargo of scotch, bourbon, and rye whiskey from one of the "Rum Row" ships. She headed

The rumrunner Lizzie D *mysteriously disappeared in 1922. Courtesy of Steve Bielenda.*

Steve Bielenda displays three types of whiskey recovered from Lizzie D's *interior: Johnny Walker scotch, on the left; Atherton bourbon, in his right hand; and Old Bridgeport rye. The wooden case has "Atherton Bourbon Whiskey, Athertonville, Kentucky, 100 Proof" burned on the side. Photo by the author.*

for Jones Inlet, *the* route during 1922 for bringing illegal alcohol from the offshore ships to the speakeasies of Manhattan.

Margaret Kerwin of Brooklyn was the tugboat's owner, and her husband was on that cruise. In 1990 their son stated that neither he nor his mother had any idea of what transpired. They only knew that *Lizzie D* had disappeared, and their father and husband had disappeared with her. His mother had been forced to wait seven years, until his father was declared legally dead, before she could collect his life insurance.

In July 1977, 55 years after *Lizzie D* sank, John Larsen, captain and owner of the dive charter boat *Deep Adventures*, discovered the wreck resting upright on the bottom. Joan Fulmer, a diver and mate on the charter boat, identified the wreck by recovering the ship's bronze bell, which had the name *Lizzie D* inscribed on it. Within her hull, the divers discovered a few skeletal remains and crates of whiskey (Johnny Walker scotch, Atherton bourbon, and Old Bridgeport rye).

The Dive. The wreck is in about 80 feet of water; the deck is reached at approximately 65 feet below the surface. There is no superstructure but the hull is relatively intact. The wooden deck planking is missing, and large openings between deck frames allow divers to penetrate the hull. A few hull plates have corroded away, allowing light penetration into some interior areas. However, digging for bottles in the silt and broken glass produces a shroud of sediment and near-zero visibility.

The four-bladed steel screw-propeller is still in place.

Artifacts. The wreck of *Lizzie D* quickly became a popular dive; since its discovery, thousands of bottles, some still containing liquor, have been recovered. Today it is rare to find an intact bottle.

Iberia

Approximate depth: 60'
Average visibility: 15'
Expertise required: Novice if visibility is good
Current/surge: Slight to moderate
Bottom: Sand and silt
Location: Three miles off Long Beach, NY
Loran numbers: 26855.3(.8) 43736.2(.3)

Launched: 1881
Sunk: November 10, 1888
Cause: Collision
Type: Passenger freighter
Length/beam: 255'/36'
Tonnage: 1,388
Condition: Flattened wreckage; bow, engine, boiler and screw-propeller are recognizable

History and sinking. Dense fog has doomed many ships; one was the passenger freighter *Iberia*. The seven-year-old French steamer was under the command of Captain Sagols when she was lost.

The Cunard luxury liner *Umbria* steamed out of New York en route to Liverpool on the morning of November 10, 1888. The damp weather was hazy and continued to thicken until the steamer was enveloped in

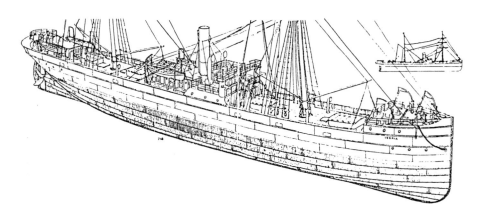

The French passenger freighter Iberia. *Courtesy of the Steamship Historical Society Collection, University of Baltimore Library.*

The Cunard liner Umbria *cuts cleanly through Iberia's hull. Courtesy of Harry Huson.*

light fog. The Cunarder, proud holder of the Atlantic "Blue Riband" maritime award for the fastest transatlantic passage, was steaming at full speed, about 19 knots. As the famous liner began her outward passage along Long Island's south shore, the fog thickened until it was impenetrable. At ten minutes after 1 p.m. Captain McMickan ordered the ship slowed down.

The Fabre Line passenger freighter *Iberia*, inbound from the Persian Gulf, shared the same pea-soup fog. The steamer had experienced engine trouble that compelled her to remain at anchor for three weeks off the Long Island shore. Captain Sagols decided to steam into shallow water, out of the heavily traveled sea lanes, and anchor there until weather conditions improved. He ordered a northward heading at three knots, and the steam whistle sounded at short intervals.

Five minutes after *Umbria*'s captain had reduced speed, he heard a steamer's whistle, which he believed to be off his starboard bow. When the sound was repeated it seemed to be nearer. Captain McMickan reacted by reducing speed again, quickly followed with an order to stop *Umbria*'s engines.

Eight minutes after McMickan's initial order for *Umbria* to slow down, *Iberia* loomed out of the fog crossing his bow. McMickan immediately ordered the engines reversed at full speed, but the liner's forward momentum drove her steel bow into the freighter's iron hull. The much larger 7,798-ton liner sliced through the 1,388-ton *Iberia* with little resistance and so little shock that few of her 711 passengers were even aware of the collision. Fourteen feet of *Iberia*'s stern drifted by Umbria's starboard bow; the bulk of the disabled *Iberia* drifted away in the opposite direction.

79

In the dense fog, it took *Umbria* 20 minutes to locate the stricken steamer. *Iberia* carried a crew of 30, but no passengers; surprisingly, there was no loss of life.

The damage to *Umbria*'s bow at the point of impact was minor. Her chief engineer was dispatched to *Iberia* to assess her damage. He found six feet of water in the engine room and she was down by what remained of the stern. He concluded that the steamer was not in immediate danger of sinking and could probably be towed into port. Both ships anchored overnight. By morning, as the fog cleared, it was evident that *Iberia* had settled further, to the point that *Umbria* could not tow her. The *Iberia*'s crew transferred to *Umbria*, and the liner returned to New York.

Two tugs were sent to tow *Iberia* to port, but before they arrived one of the steamer's bulkheads had collapsed; she had settled to the bottom with her cargo of dates, coffee, hides, and wool.

The Dive. The wreck lies on a northwest-southeast line in about 60 feet of water and is a popular dive site for novice divers. Visibility, however, can be very bad and the scattered wreckage, also a popular fishing spot, is covered with monofilament. Her engine, boiler, steel screw-propeller, and shaft are the most readily recognized parts.

Artifacts. Wood crates, some still containing dates, are occasionally recovered by divers digging in the sand.

Mistletoe

Approximate depth: 45'
Average visibility: 30'
Expertise required: Intermediate if there is little current
Current/surge: Slight to extreme
Bottom: Sand and silt
Location: 5 miles southwest of East Rockaway Inlet
Loran numbers: 26933.3 43747.6

Launched: 1872
Sunk: October 5, 1924
Cause: Fire
Type: Side-paddle wheel fishing charter boat
Length/beam: 152.6'/26.7'
Tonnage: 362
Condition: Flattened, scattered wreckage

History. By 1924 the 52-year-old side-paddle wheel steamer *Mistletoe* had outlived her usefulness as a lighthouse tender. More economical craft had taken over her task of ferrying supplies to lighthouses; the wooden-hulled steamer had been converted to use as a fishing charter vessel. This was a humiliating role for a grand side-wheeler.

Sinking. On October 5, 1924, *Mistletoe* was accommodating a group of 76 anglers, including 15 women and children. They had been fishing

The side wheeler Mistletoe. *Courtesy of the Steamship Historical Society Collection, University of Baltimore Library.*

for more than an hour when a man went below to the aft cabin for a heavier coat. He reported smoke coming from the hold. When Captain Dan Gully realized that the old wooden steamer was on fire, he ordered all passengers to the forward end of the steamer. He quickly organized a bucket brigade of the nine-man crew and nine volunteer fishermen. As they fought the spreading flames, Gully took the only fire hose below into the dense smoke and intense heat. Shortly afterward he emerged and collapsed on the deck. After being revived, he continued to help fight the fire. Despite all efforts, the fire blazed out of control. Other boats in the area quickly rescued all on board. *Mistletoe* burned to the waterline before sinking.

The Dive. Today *Mistletoe*'s paddle wheels, copper sheathing, boilers, and sundry machinery can be seen amidst her scattered ribs and planks. The walking beam engine, which operated the paddles, is lying in the sand. You can swim through the boiler and exit by the firebox.

A small piece of wreckage, south of the main site, usually harbors lobsters.

Artifacts. Captain Bill Reddan, of the charter boat *Jeanne II*, recovered a gold ring and a gold watch from this site. Brass spikes, pins, and pieces of tiles are the most recently recovered types of artifacts.

Approximate depth: 105'
Average visibility: 30'
Expertise required: Advanced
Current/surge: Slight to moderate
Bottom: Sludge, sand, and silt
Location: 10 miles south of East
Rockaway Inlet
Loran numbers: 26867.2(.6)
43670.7(.9)

Launched: 1904
Sunk: October 1, 1917
Cause: Collision
Type: Revenue cutter
Length/beam: 205'/32'
Tonnage: 980
Condition: Bow and stern are
recognizable

History. The revenue cutter _Mohawk_, named after a tribe of American Indians, was commissioned in May 1904. She was based at New York and cruised the waters between Martha's Vineyard, MA, and the Delaware breakwater. Like other vessels of the Revenue Cutter Service, she was to assist vessels in distress and enforce navigational laws.

By Act of Congress on January 30, 1915, the Revenue Cutter Service and the Life Saving Service became known as the Coast Guard Service, later the U.S. Coast Guard.

Sinking. When the United States entered World War I, _Mohawk_ and other Coast Guard vessels were temporarily transferred to the U.S. Navy. One of the duties assigned to _Mohawk_ was to patrol the approaches to

The revenue cutter Mohawk _was lost in a collision during the First World War. Courtesy of the Society for the Preservation of New England Antiquities, Boston._

New York Harbor while convoys formed before crossing the Atlantic. The cutter was performing that duty on October 1, 1917, when she was run down by the British freighter *Vennachar*. On that ill-fated morning, a cadet from the Coast Guard Academy was standing watch. *Mohawk*'s commander, First Lieutenant Iben Barker, stated he had been authorized to allow Cadet Mandeville to stand a regular watch, and as the weather was clear and all conditions favorable, he and the other officers went to breakfast.

Conditions may have been favorable, but Cadet Mandeville who had the watch apparently wasn't watching. The cadet had relieved the officer of the deck at 8 a.m. Twenty minutes later, Lt. Barker came on deck and saw a vessel of the convoy a short distance off the starboard bow, headed at right angles to their course. He knew that a collision would take place unless action were taken, and he asked Mandeville if he had sounded any signals. The cadet said no, and then blew several short blasts. By that time, however, the two vessels were already very close together. Barker rang for full speed ahead and ordered the helm hard starboard, in hopes of getting the blow as far aft as possible.

The freighter struck *Mohawk* amidships, abreast the engine room. General alarm was sounded and the cutter's pumps were started. After inspecting the engine room, Barker realized his vessel could not be saved and ordered "abandon ship." The order was executed without confusion and *Mohawk* began settling by the stern. The U.S. destroyer *Bridge* ran an 8-inch line to the cutter and secured it to the forward bitts. A code message was sent to the Convoy Commander: "Request permission to salve *Mohawk* and join convoy later." The destroyer had the cutter in tow and her engines running at one-third speed when they received an answer to their request to tow. It was disapproved. *Bridge*'s captain ordered a second request be sent, but before it could be completely transmitted it was noticed that *Mohawk* had begun to sink rapidly and list heavily to port. The tow line was cut.

With her bow high in the air, the cutter settled slowly to the bottom. Only her mastheads remained above water.

It was 9:35 a.m. when she went under. Only 20 minutes after Cadet Mandeville had gone on watch, *Mohawk* was rammed. One hour and 15 minutes later she was on the bottom. There were no casualties, and the 77 men of the cutter's crew were rescued by other naval vessels.

Mohawk was not salvaged by the Navy because the water was deemed "to deep to warrant such operations."

The Dive. The wreck site is an area often referred to by environmental groups as the "Dead Sea." For more than five decades, more than five million cubic yards of sewage sludge per year has been dumped in the area. The sludge, from the metropolitan New York area, contains high

A mound of sludge rests on Mohawk's *starboard bow. Photo by Brad Sheard.*

The skeletal remains of Mohawk's *stern. Photo by Brad Sheard.*

concentrations of organic material, bacteria, and viruses. Industrial wastes were also dumped in the area. Petroleum products and heavy metals, such as cadmium, lead, chromium, zinc, copper, nickel, and cobalt were added to the human wastes. Divers usually would visit the wreck during the late fall and early spring when the colder water might inhibit bacterial growth. Very few living marine organisms were encountered on the wreck, but the remains of fish and crabs were seen.

Biologists who studied the effects of the sludge and industrial wastes on marine life at the dump site were aghast. They applied pressure to close the site. In response, the Federal Environmental Protection Agency ordered that the dumping cease by January 1, 1982. However, the order was challenged in court by New York City's Environmental Protection Agency, one of several misnamed sewage authorities that dumped on the site. The court ruled that the dumping be continued until 1991, giving time to find land-based sites.

Environmental groups were outraged by the decision, and through their efforts the site was finally shut down in 1986. The new dumping site is on the 1,000-fathom curve, but the annual amount allowed to be dumped was increased by about 35 times.

Most divers, understandably, did not want to dive *Mohawk* and risk the unhealthy environment. However, since the dumping has ceased, the revenue cutter is slowly being scoured by currents and most of the sludge

The 6-pounder gun from this mount in Mohawk's stern was recovered by the Aquarian Dive Club, and now reposes in front of the Rockaway Coast Guard Station. Photo by Brad Sheard.

A 6-pounder deck gun, still attached to its mount, in the cutter's bow. Part of the wood deck is fastened to the gun mount's base. Photo by Brad Sheard.

A diver swims past a massive boiler that is almost covered with sludge and debris. Photo by Brad Sheard.

Artifacts recovered from Mohawk. The builder's plaque is in the back on the right. Photo by Mike deCamp.

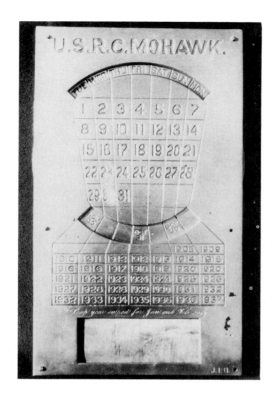

A brass calendar recovered and photographed by George Quirk.

has gone. The bottom, previously covered with several feet of sludge, has cleared to the point where the sand can be seen. Visibility, once very bad, has improved appreciably, and is now very good.

Approximately 25 feet of the cutter's bow is intact and upright. Two 6-pounder guns are partially buried in the sludge. The wreck is broken up in the midships area and the engine and four boilers can be seen amidst the debris. The deck collapsed just forward of the boilers. The stern is lying on its starboard side. Many steel plates have corroded, exposing underlying ribs. One 6-pounder deck gun is still on the stern, but only the gun mount of the other one still remains. The gun was raised by members of the Aquarian Dive Club and now reposes in front of the Rock-away Coast Guard Station.

Artifacts. Divers have recovered various artifacts, including the ship's bell, telegraphs, portholes, bronze belaying pins, case lights, gauges, bottles, and china with USRCS (U.S. Revenue Cutter Service) embossed on them. Most of the china has been recovered by digging under the decking, and pieces are still being recovered. Many artifacts, such as portholes and cage lights, are still buried in the sludge and silt.

Approximate depth: 55'
Average visibility: 10'
Expertise required: Intermediate to advanced depending upon visibility and current
Current/surge: Slight to extreme
Bottom: Silt
Location: 7½ miles southwest of East Rockaway Inlet

Loran numbers: 26936.4(9.4) 43725.5
Launched: 1943
Sunk: January 3, 1944
Cause: Explosion
Type: Destroyer
Length/beam: 348.3'/36.1'
Tonnage: 1,630
Condition: Widely scattered wreckage

History. The U.S. Navy destroyer *Turner* (DD-*648*) was named after a naval hero of the War of 1812, Captain Daniel Turner of New York. She was laid down by Federal Shipbuilding & Drydock Co. at Kearney, NJ, on November 15, 1942. Her launching took place on February 28, and she was commissioned at the New York Navy Yard on April 15, only five months after laying down. The accelerated construction program was dictated by the need to combat the challenge of Nazi Germany's U-boats.

Turner arrived at Ambrose Light at the entrance to New York Harbor late at night on January 2, 1944, midway through World War II after a convoy run from Casablanca. She anchored about six miles northeast of Sandy Hook, NJ, after having made a suspected U-boat sonar contact during the day. Her Hedgehogs were still armed. These deadly anti-U-boat weapons were mounted forward to fire a pattern of 24 rocket-launched projectiles from her bow in an attack on the site of a diving U-boat.

The U.S. destroyer Turner *was named after Captain Daniel Turner, a naval hero of the War of 1812. Courtesy of the National Archives.*

Hedgehog projectiles being loaded on spigots. Disarming projectiles like these resulted in the explosion that sank Turner. *Courtesy of the National Archives.*

Harbor security required that the Hedgehogs be disarmed before entering New York Harbor.

Sinking. Early the following morning while awaiting clearance to move into the busy harbor, a gunner's mate proceeded with the disarming. Something went wrong in the process, and at 6:18 a.m. the destroyer erupted in an explosion that was followed by an intense fire.

Turner's engine room quickly filled with smoke, but her six-man engine-room crew remained at their stations. They waited in blinding smoke for orders from the bridge, but the officers on watch were already dead, killed by the initial explosion.

Crewmen lay on deck, bleeding and in shock, some unconscious. Several others, wearing rescue breathing apparatus, rescued some of the injured personnel from the galley passageway and placed them on the fantail. Fire hoses were turned on; the first streams of water were on the blaze within three or four minutes after the explosion. But it was a futile effort.

Fortunately, several other ships were in the vicinity. Two officers on the destroyer escort *Swasey* witnessed the explosion on *Turner* and later reported "flames leaping above the *Turner* in a volcanic effect. Three projectiles that resembled rockets appeared above the flames and curved outward in wide arcs."

Within minutes, *Swasey* was under way with a fire-and-rescue team equipped and assembled on her main deck. All of her searchlights were trained upon *Turner*. The destroyer escort was maneuvered to within 20 yards of the blazing *Turner*. Her fire hoses were brought to bear on the flames, but the volume of water was pitifully ineffective for a fire of that magnitude.

Turner's entire bridge superstructure was on fire. A secondary explosion blew the number two turret end-over-end through the air, and the number one turret was forced upward and forward.

Swasey's crew discontinued their efforts to quench the flames; instead, searchlights were trained on the water to assist the small boats that were searching for survivors. Several of *Turner*'s crew had been blown into the water, others had leaped in to escape the flames. Throughout the rescue, small explosions erupted forward in the destroyer.

The U.S. Coast Guard played a major role in the rescue of the survivors who were still aboard the destroyer. One cutter came alongside the stern and took off survivors. Another Coast Guard vessel rescued 34 men from the forecastle. The cutter had just pulled away when a violent explosion, just forward of amidships, showered the Coast Guard vessel with flaming debris. It was probably the destroyer's magazine. The explosion blew *Turner*'s entire forward housing over the starboard side. The concussion blew men off their feet on nearby craft; some even lost their coats as the rush of air passed. *Turner* took a sharp list to starboard, spewing fuel oil

U.S.S. Craneship, *formerly the battleship* Kearsarge, *preparing to remove the bow and superstructure of* Turner. *This bow view of* Craneship *shows the pronounced torpedo "blisters" that were designed to absorb the impact of a torpedo hit. They also provided the old battleship with unusual stability. Courtesy of the National Archives.*

into the sea. The fuel ignited and wind fanned the flames aft. Paint caught fire, and flames ran across the decks and up her afterdeck housing. Five depth charges in a portside rack began to burn, but fortunately did not explode. However, numerous explosions, probably from 5-inch, 40mm, and 20mm ammunition, continued to punish the flaming warship.

At 7:50 a.m. a terrific explosion occurred aft of number two smokestack. The explosion was heard 30 miles away. It shattered more than 200 windows and shook houses along the Long Island and New Jersey shores.

Two hours after the initial explosion, *Turner* capsized and sank from sight. One hundred and thirty eight men died in the disaster, including 15 of the destroyer's 17 officers; only two ensigns were among the 163 survivors. About 60 would be hospitalized for months, having their wounds and burns treated. The loss of life would have been even higher except that many of the crew had left the forward mess area minutes before the initial explosion.

Turner was a navigational hazard. That prompted the U.S. Navy to demolish the wreck during the summer of 1944. U.S.S. *Craneship* used Navy divers to remove large pieces of *Turner*'s bow section and superstructure. (*Craneship* was the old battleship *Kearsarge*, stripped of her guns and equipped with a large crane mounted amidships.)

Four years later, navy divers checked the wreck's condition and found it to be "120 feet long with a highest point of about 12 feet above the ocean's bottom, which decreases to about 5 feet toward the stern. It seems to be about eight to ten feet in the sand. There is no superstructure. The wreck is on an even keel. The main deck forward is a mass of holes and is badly distorted. The deck aft is a mass of wreckage. There are numerous holes in the shell plating along both sides."

After the examination, it was determined the most economical and expeditious way to dispose of the wreck was to blast it down to sand level. The divers were directed to proceed with demolition of the wreck.

In 1976 the fully loaded supertanker *Aeolis*, drawing 48 feet of water, hit the only high point that was left on *Turner* and ripped a hole in her bottom. The tanker sank but was refloated and put back into service.

The Dive. The wreck of the destroyer lies only 55 feet under water, slightly more than 4 miles southeast of Rockaway Point. That should provide an appealing setting for sport divers. However, heavy shipping traffic and usually low visibility prevail. Steel hull plates are strewn over the bottom, but some wreckage rises about 15 feet above the sand. Captain George Quirk of the charter boat *Sea Hunter* has said that the destroyer is "the most demolished wreck I have ever seen." *Turner*'s remains more closely resemble an underwater scrap pile than the final resting place of a sleek warship that once served in the U.S. Navy.

Artifacts. Portholes, brass padlocks with "USN" engraved upon them, and china are among the artifacts that have been recovered. Captain Bill Reddan, of the charter boat *Jeanne II*, has recovered several exploded brass shell casings for the 5-inch guns. The shells probably blew up during one of several secondary explosions that occurred during the disaster. Reddan has also recovered several "torpedo bottles," old round bottomed bottles from an earlier era, indicating there may be an older wreck in the area.

Black Warrior

Approximate depth: 30'
Average visibility: 15'
Expertise required: Novice
Current/surge: Slight to extreme
Bottom: Sand and silt
Location: 6 miles west of East Rockaway Inlet
Loran numbers: 26951.8 43755.3
Launched: 1852

Sunk: February 20, 1859
Cause: Fog
Type: Side-paddle wheel passenger liner
Length/beam: 225'/37'
Tonnage: 1,5556
Condition: Scattered, flattened wreckage; engine, boiler and one paddle wheel are recognizable

History. The side-paddle wheeler *Black Warrior* precipitated a diplomatic crisis that almost developed into war with Spain. She carried passengers, mail and cargo on the New York–Havana–Mobile run for

The steamer Black Warrior *ran aground in a dense fog. Courtesy of The Mariners' Museum, Newport News, VA.*

the New York and Alabama Steamship Company. On her 18th trip to Havana, *Black Warrior* stopped to pick up supplies but did not land or load cargo. By informal arrangement with the Spanish port authorities, inspection was dispensed with on such occasions. In this instance, however, an officious Cuban port official asked for the cargo manifest. He discovered unlisted Alabama cotton aboard and detained the vessel, seized her cargo, and imposed a $6,000 fine, a considerable penalty in 1854.

The fine was paid, and *Black Warrior* was released. However, the incident generated international tension and war hysteria in the U.S., particularly in the southern states. Southerners in Congress embraced the action as justification for annexing Cuba as another slave state. Debate on the Kansas-Nebraska bill diverted legislative attention away from the explosive prospect of war with Spain.

A harshly worded protest to Madrid by the secretary of state not only failed to help, it aggravated the situation. The Spanish government still rankled from the affront by the U.S. minister to Spain, Pierre Soule, who had cosponsored the audacious Ostend Circular. The American proposition, written in Ostend, Belgium, proposed: "If Spain, actuated by stubborn pride and a false sense of honor, should refuse to sell Cuba to the United States, then . . . we shall be justified in wresting it from Spain. . . . "

The dispute worsened until Soule returned to the U.S., and less hostile minds prevailed. Spain repaid the $6,000 fine, returned the cargo, and paid an additional $53,000 as compensation for seizure of *Black Warrior*.

The ship's owners, Livingston, Crocheron & Co., moved their southern terminal from Mobile to New Orleans in 1856. The first exclusive New

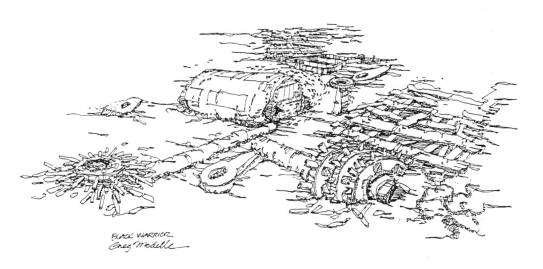

BLACK WARRIOR
Greg Modelle

Greg Modelle drew this sketch of the steamer. The most recognizable parts are the remains of the paddle wheels and the boiler.

York–New Orleans line was established and operated by the New York & New Orleans Steamship Company until the Civil War intervened.

Sinking. On February 20, 1859, the mail packet was on her way into New York Harbor with a harbor pilot aboard when she ran into a very thick fog and ran aground on Rockaway Bar. The mail and 65 passengers were transferred to the pilot boat, and two tugs were dispatched to free the side-paddle wheeler from the sandbar. One of the tugs first took off the crew, baggage, and $208,000 in currency and carried them to New York. It then returned to help the second tug in the salvage of the stranded steamer.

The vessel had grounded at high tide, and each effort to free her only settled her hull deeper into the sand. Four days later, after coal and machinery were unloaded, she finally slid off at high tide. But her freedom was short-lived; she grounded again after moving about 100 feet. Salvage efforts continued until February 27, when she was battered to pieces in a strong winter gale.

The Dive. *Black Warrior* sank about six miles west of Rockaway Inlet. As the years passed, her hull became an excellent source of blackfish for local fishermen. They noted that the inlet that used to be east of the wreck

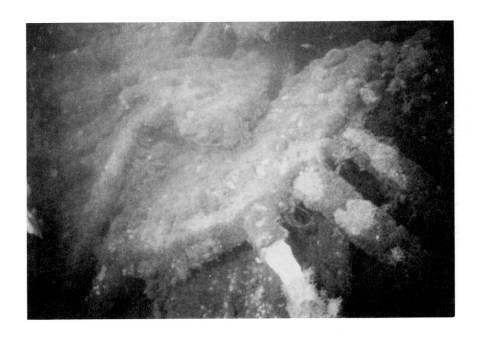

One of Black Warrior's *iron paddle-wheel hubs and spokes. Photo by Joe Bereswill.*

had gradually shifted westward until the wreck was just off the inlet. Rockaway Inlet is now stabilized with jetties.

Scuba divers have been diving the wreck since the early 1960s. It is possible to see the wreck and one of her large 32-foot-diameter wooden paddle wheels from the surface when visibility is good. One large boiler extends eight to ten feet above the bottom. Wooden timbers, decking, and metal are exposed most of the time. However, some low-lying areas may be covered by shifting sand, while other portions of the wreck are newly exposed.

Black Warrior provides an excellent dive for novice divers. Many make their first open-water dive on the wreck. An abundance of blackfish and sea bass provide inviting targets for those scuba enthusiasts who would rather spear fish than explore the historic wreckage for artifacts, and an occasional lobster is caught.

Artifacts. Identification of *Black Warrior* was confirmed by the recovery of silverware with the inscription "Black Warrior Officers." Portholes and various types of bottles have been recovered. Brass spikes and pins can still be found.

Cornelia Soule

Approximate depth: 25'
Average visibility: 15'
Expertise required: Novice if there is no surge
Current/surge: Moderate to extreme
Bottom: Sand
Location: Rockaway Shoals
Loran numbers: 26954.7 43759.1

Launched: 1885
Sunk: April 26, 1902
Cause: Ran aground
Type: Schooner
Length/beam: 123.6'/31'
Tonnage: 306
Condition: Mostly buried, with some exposed timbers and granite blocks

History and sinking. The three-masted, wooden schooner *Cornelia Soule* was loaded with eight large granite blocks intended for use as jetty stones. The 17-year-old ship was constructed by Miner & Son at Madison, CT, and was en route from Maine to Philadelphia when she encountered gale-force winds off Long Island. On April 26, 1902, the schooner ran aground on Rockaway Shoals. The schooner broke up in the heavy seas, but her crew was rescued.

The Dive. The large granite blocks are prominent amidst a few scattered planks and ribs of the schooner's wooden hull, which accounts for the wreck's title, the "Granite Wreck." The granite blocks are covered with

The schooner Cornelia Soule *ran aground on Rockaway Shoals. Courtesy of the Suffolk Marine Museum Collection, Sayville, NY.*

mussels, which attract large blackfish. The marine life and shallow depth make this an excellent dive for novices if there is good visibility and no surge.

Artifacts. The wreck is an excellent site for spearfishing, but very few artifacts are recovered. Remaining artifacts are buried in the sand.

Bronx Queen

Approximate depth: 35'
Average visibility: 20'
Expertise required: Novice if there is little or no current or surge
Current/surge: Moderate to extreme
Bottom: Sand and silt
Location: 2 miles south of Rockaway Point

Loran numbers: 26968.8 43735.1
Launched: 1942
Sunk: December 20, 1989
Cause: Struck floating object
Type: Fishing charter boat (converted submarine chaser)
Length: 110'
Tonnage: 116
Condition: The hull is intact from the engine back

History. The First World War produced 440 U.S. Navy wooden-hulled submarine chasers to cope with Germany's U-boats. One hundred of the *SC-1* design vessels were consigned to the French Navy. The 110-foot antisubmarine boats performed well for the Allies on both sides of the Atlantic.

When the war ended in 1918, the Treaty of Versailles provided for almost total disarmament of Germany. Germany was prohibited from building or otherwise acquiring submarines, but many of its most brilliant designers were kept busy on submarines in Finland, Spain, Holland, and Sweden. Adolph Hitler's repudiation of the military limitations of the Versailles Treaty was greeted with improved designs of U-boats that had been built abroad for foreign navies.

In 1937, the U.S. Navy recognized the need for new, small antisubmarine vessels similar to those developed during World War I. Another war was brewing in Europe, one that would once again demonstrate Germany's ability to devastate enemy shipping with her U-boats. The Navy's goal was a "wooden hull submarine chaser that can be constructed in from five to eight weeks on a quantity production basis for use in coastal and harbor waters and in protection of Fleet anchorages."

The new submarine chaser was an adaptation of the original *SC-1* design of World War I, with a few improvements. Hull lines aft were flattened to reduce air resistance at full speed. Increased power was achieved with two diesel engines driving triple screw-propellers in place of the three gasoline engines that drove the earlier vessels. Steel reinforcements strengthened the hull amidships and the wheelhouse was aluminum instead of wood.

The first submarine chasers were not delivered until the spring of 1942, after the United States entered World War II. By that time, U-boats had accounted for many tons of shipping sunk in American waters, almost uncontested. *SC-635* was built at the Mathis Yacht Building Company in Camden, NJ, and commissioned in October 1942. Instead of the completion target of five to eight weeks, construction of the new, 116-ton submarine chaser took more than four months. *SC-635* patrolled the eastern seaboard during the war, then was transferred to the Coast Guard when peace was restored. She was later sold, renamed *Bronx Queen*, and converted to use for fishing charters.

Sinking. The 47-year-old fishing boat was cruising off the shore of Rockaway Point, Long Island, on December 20, 1989, when she struck a floating object. Fifteen minutes later the wooden-hulled *Bronx Queen* was on the bottom. Her crew and would-be fishermen, 19 in all, treaded water in life jackets for almost two hours before they were rescued from the frigid waters. One died of exposure, another from a heart attack.

The Dive. The wreck sits upright on the bottom, but the hull forward of the engine is separated and is about 25 feet from the rest of the wreck. The engines are the highest pieces of wreckage. The stern is collapsed, but the screw-propellers are still there. Two large, square fuel tanks are in the sand on the port side.

The many large blackfish make this a good spearfishing site.

Dan Berg with the brass letters he recovered, preserved, and mounted. Photo by the author.

Artifacts. In January 1990, only one month after the sinking, Dan Berg, a veteran wreck diver/author from Baldwin, NY, visited *Bronx Queen* with several others. The group recovered a host of artifacts from the former submarine chaser, including portholes and fishing tackle.

The veteran of World War II naval service has since been wire dragged, leaving few artifacts to be found. Remaining artifacts, such as cage lights, can be found buried in the sand with only the electrical wires protruding. Most artifacts are recovered on the port side.

Unidentified Wrecks

A number of wrecks off the shores of New York and New Jersey have not yet been identified. Their names may eventually become known as divers retrieve artifacts from their remains. A capstan cover, ship's bell, or piece of china bearing the name of the vessel or the shipping line may be recovered.

Capstan covers led to the identification of *Kenosha, John C. Fitzpatrick,* and *Cornelius Hargraves.* One day we may know the names of the following unidentified wrecks:

"Seawolf" is approximately three miles south of Moriches Inlet in about 95 feet of water. It is a large steel-hulled wreck. The bow faces east, extending about 15 feet above the bottom. In other areas the hull rises only a couple of feet. A large trawler's net with floats is attached about midship. Sea bass fishermen who had lost several traps on the wreck approached Mike Casalino, of East Moriches, NY, and me in

1986. They offered the Loran numbers of the wreck (26413.2 43754.4) in exchange for retrieval of their lost traps. We gladly complied.

The Loran numbers could not be linked with any lost ship. One veteran Long Island wreck diver, Larry Listing, had the Loran numbers of a wreck in the vicinity, with the name *"Seawolf."* However, he had no record of whether it was the name for a wreck or the name of a trawler whose captain had provided the information.

The wreck is about four miles south of Moriches Inlet. Average visibility is approximately 20 feet. Advanced diving expertise is required because of the depth. Several portholes have been recovered, three in 1991.

"Walcott" is a wooden-hulled schooner in about 85 feet of water 15 miles east-southeast of Fire Island Inlet [Loran numbers 26518.1(.7) 43712.8(3.0)]. Charter boat captain Jay Porter found the wreck on July 18, 1951, the day Jersey Joe Wolcott fought Ezzard Charles for the heavyweight championship. Porter named the wreck for the victor. The wooden hull is flattened out and widely scattered and only rises a few feet off the bottom. Visibility averages about 20 feet and, because of the depth, advanced diving expertise is required.

"G & D" is in about 110 feet of water approximately 20 miles south of Fire Island Inlet [Loran numbers 26671.2(.4) 43572.7(4.3)]. The fishing charter boat captain who found the wreck named her after Gloria and Doris, two female passengers who were on board that day. The bow, the most intact part of the steel-hulled steamer, is separated from the engine and two boilers by 30 feet of sand. The stern is recognizable. Average visibility is about 30 feet, and advanced diving expertise is required.

"Dodger" is a wooden-hulled ship in about 100 feet of water, approximately ten miles south-southeast of Fire Island Inlet (Loran numbers 26617.9 43673.4). A fishing charter boat captain, Ben Letwin, named her after the baseball team because the Dodgers won the pennant on the same day he found the wreck. Flattened, low-lying wreckage with large wooden beams is all that remain. Average visibility is about 10 feet, and advanced diving expertise is required.

"59-pounder" is a wooden-hulled wreck in about 110 feet of water, so named because a cod fish of that size was caught on the wreck the day she was discovered by fishing charter boat captain Jay Porter. The wreck is approximately 17 miles southwest of Fire Island Inlet (Loran numbers 26632.4 43601.1), and all that remain are the ship's outside ribs extending about two feet above the sand. Visibility averages 30 feet, and advanced diving expertise is required. Bill deMarigny found the ship's bell, but the vessel's name was not inscribed on it.

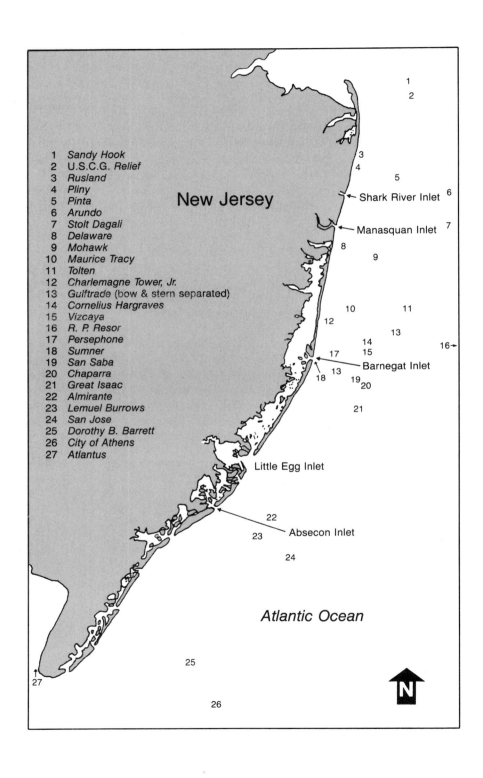

1 Sandy Hook
2 U.S.C.G. Relief
3 Rusland
4 Pliny
5 Pinta
6 Arundo
7 Stolt Dagali
8 Delaware
9 Mohawk
10 Maurice Tracy
11 Tolten
12 Charlemagne Tower, Jr.
13 Gulftrade (bow & stern separated)
14 Cornelius Hargraves
15 Vizcaya
16 R. P. Resor
17 Persephone
18 Sumner
19 San Saba
20 Chaparra
21 Great Isaac
22 Almirante
23 Lemuel Burrows
24 San Jose
25 Dorothy B. Barrett
26 City of Athens
27 Atlantus

New Jersey

Shark River Inlet

Manasquan Inlet

Barnegat Inlet

Little Egg Inlet

Absecon Inlet

Atlantic Ocean

N

3

New Jersey Shipwrecks

Approximate depth: 95'
Average visibility: 15'
Expertise required: Intermediate
Current/surge: Moderate to
  extreme
Bottom: Silt and mud
Location: Just east of Ambrose
  Light Tower
Loran numbers: 26908.2(.3)
  43700.4(.5)

Launched: 1902
Sunk: April 27, 1939
Cause: Collision
Type: Pilot boat
Length/beam: 168'/24'
Tonnage: 361
Condition: Bow and stern intact;
  midships broken up

History. Before 1854, the pilot of a ship was its steersman, the individual who conducted the navigation of a ship across the ocean and out of sight of land. The English Merchant Shipping Act of 1854 defined a pilot as being a person "duly licensed by any pilotage authority to conduct ships to which he does not belong as one of the crew. Pilots are in fact taken on board to superintend the steering of the vessel, where the navigation is difficult and dangerous, in consequence of their special knowledge of particular waters. During the period of his charge the whole responsibility of the safe conduct of the vessel devolves upon the pilot."

New York Harbor, like other major ports, has a Pilots Association to furnish pilots to inbound and outbound ships. Before the association was formed, competition between licensed pilots was fierce. They would sail their boats great distances to reach incoming ships before their competitors.

The 37-year-old steam-powered pilot boat *Sandy Hook* (Pilot Boat #2) had been built in 1902 at the Crescent Ship Yard in Elizabeth, NJ, as a private yacht. She was christened *Anstice*, and later renamed *Privateer*. In 1914, the yacht was converted into a pilot boat and named *Sandy Hook*.

The steam yacht Privateer *before conversion into a pilot boat. Courtesy of Frank Persico.*

During conversion the portholes were removed and the well deck enclosed. The pilot boat was renamed Sandy Hook. *Courtesy of Frank Persico.*

Sinking. On April 27, 1939, *Sandy Hook* was caught in a dense fog outside the entrance to New York Harbor. The 16,500-ton Norwegian liner *Oslofjord* was moving at slow speed as she neared the entrance to the harbor. Expecting a pilot boat, the liner's captain, Ole Bull, heard a whistle and ordered the engines stopped. However, the large liner's momentum carried her into the 361-ton pilot boat that had come out to meet him. The liner was hardly damaged, but the impact shattered the mast and stove in the steel hull of the pilot boat. None of the 30 men on board, including 12 pilots and several apprentices, were injured. All but six of the crew were taken off the leaking *Sandy Hook*. Then, with the pilot boat *New York* in attendance, she attempted to steam back to harbor. She foundered on the way in, but her six-man skeleton crew was taken aboard *New York*.

The Dive. The wreck site is usually referred to just as the "Pilot Boat." The bow is relatively intact and lies on its starboard side, while midships is broken up and scattered. The intact stern section rests upright on its keel. Visibility is usually poor because of the silt-and-mud bottom.

Artifacts. Captain Bill Reddan, of the charter boat *Jeanne II*, recovered three portholes and personal belongings such as a shaving kit and a mustache comb. A brass bed and several cases of 1930s Coca-Cola bottles were also recovered, and more bottles are buried in the silt and mud. An anchor, still fastened to the deck, is in the bow.

PILOT BOAT
"Sandy Hook"

Sandy Hook's wreckage was sketched by Michael Colasurdo.

U.S.C.G. *Relief* (WAL-*505*)

Approximate depth: 110'
Average visibility: 20'
Expertise required: Advanced
Current/surge: Moderate to
 extreme
Bottom: Sand, silt, and mud
Location: 1 mile southeast of the
 Ambrose Light Tower

Loran numbers: 26903.5
 43695.6(.9)
Launched: 1904
Sunk: June 24, 1960
Cause: Collision
Type: Lightship
Length/beam: 129'/28.6'
Tonnage: 566
Condition: Intact hull

History. The ship channel to the heavily traveled entrance of New York Harbor is guarded by the famous Ambrose Light. Its familiar beacon is a welcome navigational aid to seamen at night and in bad weather. Seamen have always dreaded the area during periods of dense fog, particularly with ships converging there to enter or exit the harbor. The light now beams from a stationary tower structure that was constructed in 1967. Up until that time, the U.S. Coast Guard lightship *Ambrose* (WAL-*213*) lay anchored in the center of the entrance to the channel. The ship carried two powerful beacons, a foghorn, and a radio.

In June 1960, the Coast Guard lightship *Relief* (WAL-*505*) temporarily replaced *Ambrose* so that the latter could undergo routine maintenance.

The lightship had her name lettered in white on both sides of the red hull.
Courtesy of Steve Bielenda.

Sinking. In the predawn hours of June 24, the freighter *Green Bay* was leaving the harbor en route to Ethiopia. The freighter was shrouded in dense fog, slowly steaming through the Ambrose ship channel, staying to the center and deep water. Captain Thomas Mazzella knew the lightship was anchored in the center of the channel. It never occurred to him to consider the lightship anything but a welcome aid in foul weather conditions, certainly not a hazard. He felt comfortable hearing the lightship's foghorn sound her position at the end of the channel.

Captain Mazzella picked up *Relief* on radar, but he miscalculated the distance between the two vessels, which he thought was a mile and a half. When he felt sure that he was out of the narrow ship channel, he ordered a slight change in course and increased speed. He walked out on the wing bridge to assist his lookouts in their search for the lightship's fog-dimmed beacon. Abruptly, *Relief*'s red steel hull loomed directly ahead. Mazzella shouted an order to reverse engines, but it was too late.

The coastguardsman on duty on the lightship's bridge first saw the freighter at a distance of only 50 feet. He immediately sounded the general alarm to rouse the eight men sleeping below. The freighter struck the lightship on her starboard side just aft of amidships. The lightship's crew, still groggy after being awakened by the alarm, were flung from their bunks by the impact. The lightship rolled 15 degrees to port, then righted herself. There were no serious injuries or fatalities. The only loss was the lightship.

The coastguardsmen inflated a rubber life raft and abandoned ship. The freighter, only slightly damaged, dropped anchor and launched her lifeboats to pick up the crew of the stricken vessel. They were transferred to another vessel and the freighter continued her voyage. That afternoon, the lightship *Ambrose* was prematurely put back on station, and a buoy

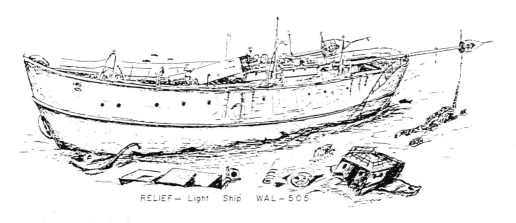

RELIEF — Light Ship WAL — 505

The lightship's wreckage was sketched by Michael Colasurdo before the lights were recovered by divers.

In 1974, members of the Aquarian Dive Club recovered the brass plaque that was placed on the lightship when the Maryland Drydock Co. dieselized the vessel in 1935.
Photo by Val Ackins.

Artifacts recovered from Relief. Photo by Michael deCamp.

was placed over the wreck to identify *Relief* as a hazard to navigation. The wreck was later wire-dragged, destroying the superstructure and tearing off her masts. Then, the buoy was removed.

The Dive. The wreck, usually referred to as the "Lightship," sits upright on the bottom; the deck is about 70 feet below the surface. The bottom is sand, silt, and mud and when disturbed lessens visibility. Less experienced divers should remain on the deck where visibility is usually better.

The hull remains intact, but several square openings in the deck allow divers to penetrate and swim from one end to the other. However, like most wrecks, considerable sediment within lessens visibility when it is disturbed.

Artifacts. In the stern, where the officers' quarters were located, Captain Bill Reddan of the charter boat *Jeanne II* recovered binoculars with "USCG" printed on them, as well as charting equipment.

In July, 1991, Captain Frank Persico of the charter boat *Sea Hawk* found a complete porthole lying in the sediment in the ship's galley. The porthole's rim was bent into a "V" shape, probably during the collision that sank the lightship, but the glass swingplate was undamaged. Several brass porthole rims, without their glass swingplates, are still attached to the hull. Divers attaching a swim line to the wreckage and then searching the surrounding sand have found old whiskey and beer bottles.

The lightship's bell was recovered by the Aquarian Dive Club. Photo by Val Ackins.

Approximate depth: 25'
Average visibility: 10'
Expertise required: Novice if
  there is no surge or current
Current/surge: Slight to extreme
Bottom: Sand
Location: 200 feet off
  Long Branch, NJ
Loran numbers: 26950.2 43598.8

Launched: 1872
Sunk: March 17, 1877
Cause: Ran aground
Type: Passenger liner
Length/beam: 345'/37.1'
Tonnage: 2,538
Condition: Flattened, scattered
  wreckage

History. The remains of two ships are scattered over the bottom of the same area, about 200 feet off Long Branch, NJ. The site is commonly referred to as the "Dual Wrecks."

The Dutch bark *Adonis* ran aground off Long Branch while battling a gale on March 7, 1859. The 550-ton sailing vessel was loaded with a cargo of lead ingots and mill grindstones, each weighing more than 400 pounds. The wooden-hulled ship could not be refloated, and broke up during a subsequent storm. Eighteen years later, on March 17, 1877, the iron-hulled Red Star liner *Rusland* reached the same location, driven by a northeast gale. The passenger liner was headed for New York Harbor with 125 passengers — five cabin class and 120 steerage Italian, German, and French immigrants from Antwerp, Belgium. The ship carried a $200,000 cargo that included wines, window and plate glass, a case of oil paintings, 12 cases of zinc, church ornaments, and 1,000 packages of iron wire.

The British single-screw, brig-rigged steamer *Rusland* was built in Dundee, Scotland, in 1872 and christened *Kenilworth*. She was later sold

The Red Star passenger liner Rusland *ran aground in 1877. Courtesy of The Mariners' Museum, Newport News, VA.*

to the Red Star Line and renamed *Rusland*. *Kenilworth*'s first officer, Jesse De Horsey, was promoted to captain of *Rusland*. It was his first command; his new ship's maiden voyage for her new owners was her last.

Sinking. On March 15, 1859, the steamer took on a pilot 100 miles off Long Island. Private pilots traveled such distances to meet incoming ships to beat their competitors. However, the pilot was not to take command until the ship reached the entrance to the harbor. Captain De Horsey remained in command until then, compensating for the gale-force wind and tide with a course set half a point to windward.

Soundings were taken as the liner neared land. Both captain and pilot agreed that they were still off Long Island and were keeping a sharp watch for Fire Island Light. At 10:30 p.m., the lookout called out a warning, "Light on the port bow!" De Horsey instinctively took it to be another ship because the lighthouse he was expecting should have been on his starboard. When land appeared on the port bow, he ordered the vessel to be put about, but the liner grounded bow on with so slight an impact that he could barely feel it. He remarked to the pilot, "That was a close shave," but within seconds he realized that the liner was hard aground. She resisted all efforts to back her off.

De Horsey ordered that sleeping cabin passengers should not be awakened because the ship was in no immediate danger. However, some

Passengers being rescued from the stranded Rusland. *The men on the right are pulling the lifesaving car to shore. Courtesy of* Harper's Monthly.

of the steerage passengers who had felt the grounding became so agitated that the captain ordered passageways to the steerage quarters locked "to prevent the people from coming on deck and making trouble."

Distress rockets alerted the crews of two lifesaving stations to the plight of the stranded vessel. Heavy seas complicated rescue operations, but by 4 a.m. a line had been fired from a Lyle gun on shore and attached high on a mast. The slow work of landing the passengers commenced, with a two-seat lifesaving car suspended from a pulley on a line between shore and ship. The ride was a harrowing experience for the passengers, particularly for the overweight who caused the line to sag. Passengers were not only carried over, but, at times, through the booming surf to the beach. Some of them were transported ashore in lifeboats, another difficult task. It took six hours to transfer all the passengers, while the crew moved baggage from the lower to the main deck, then sent it ashore on the lifesaving car. That afternoon, when De Horsey came ashore with his crew, he was surprised to learn that he had landed in New Jersey. Until then, he believed that he had grounded on Fire Island.

Salvors from a salvage vessel that had been dispatched to the scene found about 15 feet of water in the aft hold. *The New York Times* treated the salvage effort as a social event, reporting, "Everybody in Long Branch turned out yesterday and today to see the *Rusland*, where she lay off the shore at the East End, and wagons of all kinds brought visitors from outlying villages. These thronged the beach and watched the vessel until the icy wind drove them to shelter."

The heavy seas swung the liner broadside to the beach and exposed her to crashing waves that cloaked her in clouds of spray from stem to stern. When wind and sea had subsided, *Rusland*'s hull was examined. It had been torn open by the grindstones that *Adonis* had been carrying when she sank 18 years earlier. *Rusland* had grounded precisely on top of the sunken Dutch bark, parts of which were still visible at low tide.

Water inside the British liner's hull rose and fell with the changing tides. One old salt watching from the beach expressed his opinion of the possibility of salvage: "You might as well try to pump the sea dry, as that vessel." He was proven correct when a survey by two divers revealed that the ship could not be refloated.

Cargo in the forward hold that had hardly been touched by water was salvaged. Western Union installed a telegraph line from shore to the wreck to allow the steamer's agents in New York and Philadelphia to communicate with the salvors. While the salvage was continuing, *Rusland* rested heavily on *Adonis*, crushing the old ship's timbers and ribs. Wooden debris was strewn for miles along the shore. Severe storms interfered with the cargo salvage; little more than half was saved. The iron hull eventually broke up.

The Dive. Access to the wreck should be by boat despite its proximity to shore. The adjacent land is privately owned, so most divers visit the

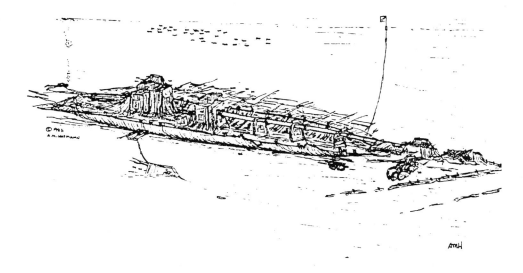

The "Dual Wrecks" were sketched by Al Hofmann. The outline of Adonis' wooden hull and her grindstones are at the right.

site from a charter boat. In return, they get two wrecks for the price of one. The more recent *Rusland* is represented by her iron hull plates, boiler tubes, engine, and prop shaft. Blended with her remains, huge grindstones from *Adonis* are scattered in the sand amidst a few wooden ribs and timbers that extend up about six inches.

This site is good for spearfishing and for finding lobsters.

Artifacts. One-hundred-and-fifteen-pound lead ingots and bronze fastenings of the old wooden schooner are occasionally recovered. In 1991, two portholes, a couple of valves, and some anchor chain were recovered from the passenger liner.

Pliny

Approximate depth: 20'
Average visibility: 10'
Expertise required: Novice if there is no surge
Current/surge: Slight to extreme
Bottom: Sand
Location: Off Deal Casino in Deal, NJ
Loran numbers: 26949.2 43579.8

Launched: 1878
Sunk: May 13, 1882
Cause: Ran aground
Type: Passenger freighter
Length/beam: 288'/33'
Tonnage: 1,671
Condition: Some pieces extend six feet above the bottom

History and sinking. The passenger freighter *Pliny* left Rio de Janeiro on April 22, 1882, for New York, carrying 21 passengers and a crew of 34. Her cargo consisted of 20,000 bags of coffee and 500 bales of hides.

The passenger freighter Pliny *aground off Deal, NJ. Courtesy of The Mariners' Museum, Newport News, VA.*

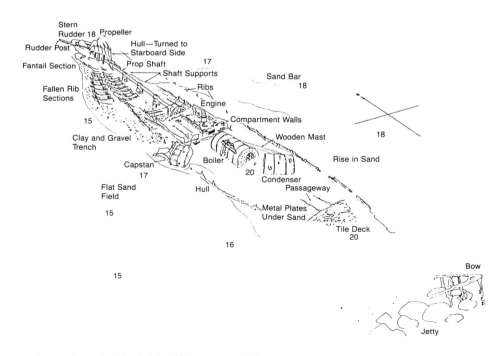

Dan Lieb made this sketch of Pliny *about 1980.*

On May 13, she was shrouded in fog and battling gale-force winds when she ran aground off Deal, NJ. Heavy seas pounded the stranded ship, quickly driving her parallel to the beach. Water cascaded over her decks, washing away hatch covers and pouring into the holds below. Captain Robert Mitchell fired distress rockets. Though the crew of the nearby lifesaving station was off duty, it assembled with rescue equipment by dawn. A Lyle gun was fired to carry a breeches buoy line to the ship, and the rescue team manned surfboats.

Everyone aboard was rescued, but not before crewmen broke into the ship's wine storage compartment. Their attack on the fine wines left them less concerned for their survival, and of little help in the rescue. Several fell into the sea trying to enter the surfboats. One or two were so drunk when they reached the beach that they had to be assisted to the lifesaving station. *Pliny* broke in two the following day from the pounding of the heavy seas on the steamer's steel hull.

The Dive. The twisted steel wreckage lies in ten to 20 feet of water off Ocean Ave. in front of the Deal Casino in Deal, NJ. The casino is a private club, and access to the beach is prohibited to all but members. Local police are particularly strict about parking in the adjacent streets. Diving from a boat is always permitted and is the recommended approach. The best time for diving the wreck is at high tide and when there is no surge.

Artifacts. An 1880s passenger freighter should produce many interesting artifacts, such as china, silverware, bottles, serving trays, and so forth. This wreck, however, is not a productive site for artifacts. Many must still be buried in the sand.

Pinta

Approximate depth: 90'
Average visibility: 20'
Expertise required: Intermediate
Current/surge: Slight to moderate
Bottom: Sand and clay
Location: 8 miles east northeast of Shark River Inlet
Loran numbers: 26880.5 43563.5(4.1)

Launched: 1959
Sunk: May 7, 1963
Cause: Collision
Type: Freighter
Length/beam: 194'/31'
Tonnage: 500
Condition: Intact except for the wheelhouse

History and sinking. The 500-ton Dutch freighter *Pinta* was en route from Central American ports to New York Harbor with a cargo of lumber on May 7, 1963. At the same time, the British freighter *City of Perth*

The Dutch freighter Pinta *was run down by the British freighter* City of Perth. *Courtesy of The Mariners' Museum, Newport News, VA.*

was outbound from New York to Australia. Both ships were equipped with radar and the weather was clear, with visibility of 15 miles. Under those ideal conditions, the British vessel rammed *Pinta* on her port side at 7:59 p.m., one minute past official sunset. The prow of the 7,547-ton ship easily sliced through the smaller ship's steel hull. Both took on water and radioed for Coast Guard assistance. *Pinta*'s crew abandoned her as she listed to port, and transferred to the British freighter. The Dutch freighter sank within 48 minutes.

City of Perth suffered a 14-foot gash in her stem, but she managed to steam back to New York for repairs in dry dock. Although the circumstances invited inquiry, there was no Coast Guard investigation of the accident because it involved two foreign-flag vessels in international waters, outside the service's jurisdiction.

The Dive. Five months after *Pinta* settled to the bottom, 13 members and guests of the Oceanographic Historical Research Society, a group of pioneer wreck divers from New York, made the first dive to the new wreck. They had tried to visit the site sooner, but could not find a boat captain to take them out, and then there were weather delays. They finally anchored over the wreck on October 5, 1963, aboard a chartered fishing boat. The captain took only three passes to find the wreck.

The initial reaction of the divers as they hit the water was disappointment. They dove into a muddy brown sea that led them to expect minimal visibility. But as they descended the anchor line, the water cleared, and at 15 feet below the surface *Pinta* loomed sharp but dark in crystal clear water. She lay on her port side, completely intact, her hull only 50 feet deep.

Mike deCamp, a veteran wreck diver and underwater photographer from Morristown, NJ, later described the initial dive in *Skin Diver* magazine: "The descent was like moving from a small, dark closet into a vast open courtyard. Soon the bridge and superstructure came into sharp relief, while in the dusky distance and across the sand trailed masts and rigging in a phantom array. . . . The water was so clear and the ship so

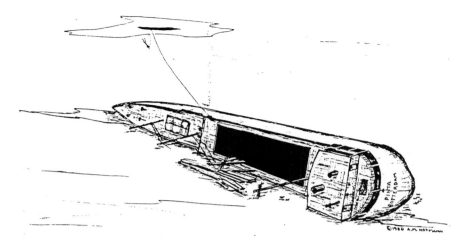

Pinta*'s wreckage was sketched by Al Hofmann.*

Pinta*'s bell before recovery. Photo by Michael deCamp.*

intact that the sudden freedom of the diver gave one the feeling of a glider in a dream world. We rounded the stern to find darkly embossed against the white hull the words, PINTA ROTTERDAM."

Word of the dive spread rapidly through the diving community. Of a second dive, deCamp wrote: "The ship could be entered from a number of points. . . . Inside were a great array of tools neatly hung and ready for use. On the bottom side of the bridge lying three feet off the sand a broken glass window gave access to the bridge. Inside the bridge was a big table with drawers which when opened upside down gave forth a shower of flags. Among them was a flag with a big "D" for the Dovar Line and another long flag with the word PINTA. . . . "

Pinta's name on the stern is barely recognizable now; the hull is almost completely covered by marine growth. The freighter, lying on her port side, is still intact except for the wheelhouse, a pleasant surprise for divers in the area. Most local shipwrecks have been ravaged by time and

A diver by Pinta*'s screw-propeller. Photo by Michael deCamp.*

the sea or by man's efforts to rid the waters of a navigational hazard. *Pinta* is a welcome exception. She awaits divers who want to view an example of how Hollywood might portray an underwater wreck. They are not disappointed.

The wreck today is considered to be a good lobster dive. As it is almost intact, it is also ideal for photography.

Artifacts. The divers recovered many artifacts on the initial dive, but the most prized was the one that was brought to the surface by Jack Brewer, one of the guest divers. His ever-to-be treasured artifact was the ship's bronze bell bearing the inscription "PINTA 1959."

Two of the divers found a box of business cards with the name "Captain Arie Korpelshoek" in a drawer in the captain's cabin. In addition, deCamp recovered a small box of foreign and American coins and bills.

Few artifacts are recovered now.

Arundo

Approximate depth: 125'
Average visibility: 20'
Expertise required: Advanced
Current/surge: Slight to moderate
Bottom: Sand and mud
Location: 16 miles east of Shark River Inlet
Loran numbers: 26796.3(.6)(.9) 43533.9(4.4)(4.8)

Launched: 1930
Sunk: April 28, 1942
Cause: Torpedo
Type: Freighter
Length/beam: 412'/55.3'
Tonnage: 5,079
Condition: Some areas are partially intact, lying on their starboard side

History. Winston Churchill's term for one of the most decisive military conflicts in the history of warfare was the "Battle of the Atlantic," the confrontation that pitted Germany's World War II submarine fleet against Britain, Canada, and the United States. He wrote in *The Second World War*: "The only thing that ever really frightened me during the war was the U-boat peril . . . I was even more anxious about this battle than I had been about the glorious air fight called the 'Battle of Britain.'"

Germany's ally, Japan, struck Pearl Harbor on the morning of December 7, 1941; Congress declared war the next day. On December 11, Germany declared war. Then followed a period of frustration for the United States; its naval forces could not deal with the U-boat menace for months after her entry into the conflict. Churchill observed that those U-boat successes threatened the Allied war effort more than decimation of the American battle fleet at Pearl Harbor. During the six months that followed, more than three million tons were destroyed by Germany's underwater fleet. Most were sunk in American waters. One was the Dutch freighter *Arundo*, torpedoed near the Ambrose Lightship on April 28, 1942, by Korvetten-kapitan Zimmerman in *U-136*.

Arundo was built in 1930 at Newcastle, England, for Woodfield Shipping Company and christened *Petersfield*. The ship was sold to B.J. Sutherland and Company in 1936, and was renamed *Cromarty*. She was later sold to N.V. Maats Zeevaart of Rotterdam, Holland, and her name was changed for the last time.

Sinking. The freighter was placed under charter to the British Ministry of War Transport. She was en route from New York to Alexandria, Egypt, on April 28, 1942, with a cargo that included 4,545 drums of lubrication oil, 54,711 bags of nitrate, two train locomotives, and their tenders. She also carried 123 1½-ton Ford trucks and other war material destined to help check Rommel's sweep across North Africa. Less military supplies, such as 4,995 cases of Canadian beer, 6,844 cases of canned herring in

Arundo just before her final voyage. Note the two locomotives lashed to the deck by the aft mast. Courtesy of the U.S. Coast Guard.

tomato sauce, and 2,000 cases of evaporated milk, were also included. The locomotives, tenders, and a number of trucks were secured on deck; the remaining cargo was stowed in the Dutch freighter's holds.

At 9:30 a.m., *Arundo* was steaming at full speed, ten knots, but not zigzagging, with three officers and one seaman on the bridge and one lookout aft. The weather was clear, the sea calm with slight swells, and visibility excellent. The freighter was not in convoy, but two tankers and a U.S. destroyer were about four miles to the south. Chief Officer Akkerman, off watch at the time, was standing on deck enjoying the warmth of the early morning spring sun when he saw a torpedo track, a white streak of turbulent water three feet wide, off the starboard beam. The torpedo struck amidships beneath the bridge. The explosion was not loud, but a violent concussion shook the freighter from stem to stern. A high column of water erupted on the starboard side. The steel hull in the area of the number-two hold was extensively damaged and hatch covers were blown off. The steamer developed a sharp starboard list of almost 90 degrees, and sank by the bow within five minutes.

The large freighter was armed with a 4-inch deck gun mounted on the poop deck, two twin Marlin machine guns (a modified Colt M 1895 gun) just forward of the deck gun, two 20mm anti-aircraft guns mounted on the port side of the chart room, and two 30-caliber Hotchkiss machine guns mounted on the bridge wings. However, defensive action was out of the question because the submerged U-boat was never sighted.

The freighter carried a complete set of British Navy codes and decoding tables. They, along with other confidential papers, were kept in a perforated steel box that was locked in the chart room at the time of the attack; it went down with the ship.

The crew abandoned ship in lifeboats and rafts that had not been destroyed in the blast. Two of the lifeboats were damaged in launching and one was pulled under when the ship sank. Thirty-seven men were rescued later by the U.S. destroyer *Lea*, but six others were lost in the disaster. They may have been pulled under with the lifeboat, or crushed by one of the locomotives toppling into the water amidst the swimming survivors. The destroyer searched for the U-boat for two hours without success before coming to the rescue of the survivors. Less than three months later, Zimmerman and U-*136* were less fortunate; the U-boat was lost off Spain in an attack on an Allied convoy.

News of *Arundo*'s loss was withheld from the public by the United States government to avoid acknowledging the presence of U-boats in U.S. coastal waters.

The Dive. The freighter and her mixed cargo were left undisturbed until 1950, when the vessel was blown apart with explosives and wire dragged to a depth of 72 feet.

Several wrecks lie in the vicinity of *Arundo*'s reported sinking. Fishing charter boat captains were never certain which wreck was the Dutch freighter. They named the various remains according their depth, always on the assumption that it was *Arundo*: the 120-foot *Arundo*, the 130-foot *Arundo*, the 140-foot *Arundo*. The speculation ended in 1966 when Evelyn Dudas of West Chester, PA, recovered the artifact most treasured by divers, the ship's bronze bell. It bore the ship's original name *Petersfield*.

Although the wreck was blown apart and wire dragged to destroy it as a navigational hazard, a few sections are relatively intact, allowing penetration. Remains of the Ford trucks abound. Truck bodies are decomposed, but chassis, axles, differentials, engines, and tires are scattered throughout the wreckage. Many tires, mounted on rims, are still stacked neatly together in racks.

The locomotives are somewhat difficult to locate. The engineer cabs and most other sections except boilers and wheels have oxidized away. Poor visibility and disorientation on the wreck contribute to the difficulty in finding them. The two locomotives are in sand on the starboard side about 75 feet forward of the massive screw-propeller. One is almost completely obscured under debris, lying on its side next to the outside bulkhead of the aftermost hold; the only parts that are easily recognized are the small front wheels.

Arundo is one of the largest wrecks off the New Jersey shore. Her wreckage is scattered over a broad area, producing a vast artificial reef that is excellent for spearfishing, catching lobsters, or gathering artifacts. However, there is a large trawler's net on part of the wreck.

Artifacts. After the war the Diamond Salvage Co. of Washington wanted to raise *Arundo* to recover a shipment of "valuable instruments," which they did not further identify. In November 1945, their divers surveyed the wreck and concluded that *Arundo* could not be raised.

One item of cargo that has survived *Arundo*'s decades under the sea is quart-size Canadian beer bottles. They are the most frequently recovered artifacts. The remains of the helm, still attached to the stand, was lying in the sand in 1991.

Stolt Dagali

Approximate depth: 130'
Average visibility: 30'
Expertise required: Intermediate to advanced
Current/surge: Slight to extreme
Bottom: Sand
Location: 17 miles east of Manasquan Inlet
Loran numbers: 26787.6(8.0) 43484.3(.4)

Launched: 1955
Sunk: November 26, 1964
Cause: Collision
Type: Tanker
Length/beam: 582.5'/70.9'
Tonnage: 12,723
Condition: Stern section only, but virtually intact

History and sinking. The luxury cruise ship *Shalom*, newest and fastest of Israel's merchant fleet, left New York late on Thanksgiving Eve November 25, 1964. She was on her maiden cruise, bound for the sunny Caribbean. Three hours later, sea conditions changed abruptly from clear skies with wind and heavy seas to an impenetrable wall of fog. *Shalom*'s captain made no effort to reduce the new liner's 20.5 knots speed. Neither did he post a lookout.

The 616 passengers had been celebrating their departure for warmer climes with usual shipboard abandon. By about 2 a.m., the party had begun to wind down. Many of the passengers had retired when the ship shuddered, signalling an impact. Many sleeping passengers were unaware that anything was wrong. Those who were still celebrating realized that something unusual had occurred.

Ship's officers reassured the concerned passengers, but something had indeed gone wrong. The speeding cruise ship had struck the Norwegian tanker *Stolt Dagali* and sliced cleanly through her. The nine-year-old tanker's amputated stern, with 19 of her crew, sank within minutes. Watertight compartments kept her 44-foot bow and amidships afloat. The section was towed back to New York, where the bow was later refitted with a new stern, allowing the tanker to return to service.

Twenty-four crew members survived. Some were on the bow section; others had been thrown into the sea from their stern quarters when the ship was cut in two. They were rescued by the Coast Guard and boats from *Shalom*. Thirteen bodies were later recovered.

Dagali is the name of a Norwegian town for which the tanker was named. *Stolt Dagali* means "Pride of Dagali," but the pride of Dagali was now in two parts, a dismembered symbol of marine disaster. The tanker had been en route from Philadelphia to Newark with a cargo of industrial solvents and vegetable oil when she was struck.

It is surprising that the collision occurred. Both vessels were equipped with radar and it was in use. Minutes before his ship was cut in two, the

The Norwegian tanker Stolt Dagali. *Courtesy of Tom Roach.*

The tanker's stern was sheared off when she was rammed by the Israeli luxury liner Shalom. *The bow, which remained afloat, was towed as shown in this photo. U.S. Coast Guard photo courtesy of William Quinn.*

tanker's captain, Kristian Bendiksen, said he stared at his radarscope in disbelief. He could not conceive "that any ship could come so close so fast up to us." When the radar showed the cruise ship within two miles, Bendiksen said he expected the other ship to take evasive action.

When *Shalom* approached to within six-tenths of a mile, the tanker's second mate heard a whistle followed by, "I can see the loom of lights . . . ship is heading right on us." By then the distance had narrowed to four-tenths of a mile. Bendiksen then ordered full speed ahead and rudder hard aport.

The Zim Line, *Shalom*'s owners, blamed the captain of the tanker for the disaster. Their representatives claimed that Bendiksen had seen the cruise ship on his radar and moved directly across the cruise ship's bow. If the tanker had held to her course, the ships would have passed safely according to their testimony.

Captain Avner Freudenberg of *Shalom* said he returned to the bridge when he was informed of the fog. A watch officer pointed to the image of a ship on the radarscope 1⁴⁄₁₀ miles away. Freudenberg later admitted that he did not reduce speed until 90 seconds before the collision. He did, however, order the foghorn to be sounded.

A court of inquiry found both ships partially responsible for the collision. *Shalom*'s captain failed to slow his ship appreciably and did not have a lookout posted. The ship's primary radar was not functioning well. The radarscope was cluttered by interference, and the officer on watch failed to switch on the backup unit. *Stolt Dagali*'s captain failed to plot the course of the approaching cruise ship. Instead of waiting to see what the other ship would do, he could have taken evasive action.

On the day after the sinking, Mike deCamp, a veteran diver from New Jersey, and several associates chartered the *Daisy B*, operated by scuba diver Jack Brown, in an unproductive search for the wreck. They gave up but returned two days later for another attempt, which was aborted by high seas. Brown and deCamp would not be deterred; the next day

121

Carl Helwick recovered the tanker's elaborate, brass builder's plaque. Courtesy of Steve Bielenda.

A diver inspects a large white "S" on a black flag painted on the tanker's smoke stack. Photo by Michael deCamp.

they joined Jim Caldwell of Ocean City, NJ, on a charter aboard *Albatross III* although the weather had not improved appreciably in 24 hours. In an article for *Skin Diver*, deCamp wrote: "The pilothouse and the deck were awash with spray as the boat took white water over the bow. All hands had to hang on as we plowed directly into the gathering northeaster."

The divers were determined to locate the wreck and photograph it. They knew it would be several days before the weather would allow another try. That convinced them to continue. Luck favored them when they sighted an oil slick a few miles short of the reported wreck site, and followed it directly to the sunken tanker.

Robin Palmer, from New York City, and deCamp went over the side first. According to deCamp's account, "The calm water below was a relief from the tossing struggle topside, and after a drop of 30 feet the stark white hull glittered below us. We landed very close to where the ship was sliced, an indescribable mess of sheared and twisted metal. . . . We worked our way . . . over to the huge smokestack with the big "S" on it. Past porthole and skylight we curved downward to the name on the stern at a depth of 110 feet. The name was so large that only an S and a T could be brought into the frame of the camera."

Brown and two other divers, Caldwell and Russel Koch, entered the engine room and worked their way down several passageways. They shared a common dread that they would encounter the remains of some of the crew whose bodies had not been recovered. They were spared that trial. One of the divers, Jack Brewer, from Easton, PA, shot film that was later featured on ABC and NBC News.

The divers negotiated a contract with *Shalom*'s owners to determine the position of the tanker's rudder and engine room telegraph. They intended to use the information in determining fault in the accident. The divers returned to the wreck on December 21 and, in the course of that dive, they did encounter a corpse; they retrieved the body of a stewardess who had been trapped in the laundry room.

The Dive. The tanker is, and has been since her sinking, one of the most popular and regularly visited wrecks off the New Jersey coast. The 142-foot stern section, containing the engine room and crew's quarters, is virtually intact. There is an added attraction in the choice of depth, which ranges from 70 to 130 feet for various parts of the wreck. The wreck is affectionately referred to as the "Stolt." It is an excellent lobster source.

The stern, lying on its starboard side, is virtually intact and, with the good visibility that usually prevails, it provides many opportunities for the underwater photographer. The smokestack is prominent as it juts out over the sand. However, the large "S" is no longer visible. Like the rest of the wreck, it is obscured by the marine organisms that cover the artificial reef.

Many openings allow penetration. A large skylight just forward of the stack offers entry into the engine room. The passageways are wide, but penetration should be approached with caution. Specialized training and equipment are essential.

Bart Malone, a veteran wreck diver from Bellmawr, NJ, stated that "when swimming through passageways, the diver is descending from

A diver prepares to photograph Stolt's *mast lights. Photo by Michael deCamp.*

about 70 feet to approximately 95 feet. Often divers do not realize the change in depth." In the washout by the screw-propeller, a diver may reach a depth of 135 feet.

Artifacts. Interesting artifacts are still occasionally recovered at the wreck site. In 1990, veteran wreck divers Scott Jenkins and Dave McFadden retrieved eight silver serving trays, eight china dinner plates, and silverware, all bearing the ship's insignia in gold. Exploring the same location — the officer's dining area — other divers were rewarded on the same day with salt and pepper shakers and a crystal plate.

Delaware

Approximate depth: 70'
Average visibility: 15'
Expertise required: Intermediate
Current/surge: Moderate to extreme
Bottom: Sand
Location: 2.6 miles south of Manasquan Inlet
Loran numbers: 26928.4 43467.5

Launched: 1880
Sunk: July 9, 1898
Cause: Fire
Type: Passenger freighter
Length/beam: 251.7'/37'
Tonnage: 1,646
Condition: Very little of the wood hull is left in the stern, the bow is more intact

The wooden passenger freighter Delaware, *burned and sank in 1898. Courtesy of The Mariners' Museum, Newport News, VA.*

History. The Clyde Line passenger freighter *Delaware* had served in the company's West Indies service, primarily as a freighter. She was forced into coastal passenger service during the Spanish-American War, while larger Clyde Line passenger liners were being used as transports to carry American troops to Cuba.

Sinking. *Delaware* left her New York pier beneath the Brooklyn Bridge at 3:30 p.m. on July 8, 1898. The wooden steamship was bound for South Carolina and Florida ports with 32 passengers and a general cargo. Captain A.D. Ingram's crew consisted of 32 men and a stewardess.

The steamship passed through the waters off Sandy Hook in a calm sea under clear skies. The shore was lined with menacing fortifications, and the water was mined to protect against intrusion by Spanish naval forces. By 9:30 p.m., most of the passengers who had viewed the passing scene of their first day at sea from on deck had retired.

At about 10:00 p.m., the officer on the bridge was informed of smoke from the aft cargo hatch. The crew attacked the fire with axes, cutting into the deck to insert fire hoses, but the flames and heat continued to mount. Additional holes only increased the volume of smoke that billowed out of the ship's hold, prompting Captain Ingram to alert the passengers to the danger.

The first officer and the stewardess moved quietly from one stateroom to another, informing passengers that there was a fire aboard, and that they were to come on deck as a precautionary measure. Most dressed quickly but others, not fully reassured, dashed out of their staterooms in nightclothes. Crewmen guided the confused passengers through smoke-filled passageways to the deck above. There were anxious moments for those who were aware of the fact that *Delaware* was carrying ammunition in her cargo holds.

At the time the fire was discovered, the steamer was about ten miles off Bay Head, NJ. Captain Ingram headed for shore immediately, but by the time the ship was about two miles offshore, the blaze had burned through the deck in several places. Rocket flares were fired to attract the attention of nearby vessels.

Captain Ingram realized that his ship could not be saved and ordered it abandoned. Nine women and four children entered the lifeboats first, followed by the stewardess. A bride remained behind with her husband to wait for another boat. Two male Cuban nationals created a scene when they tried to force their way into the boat. They were forcibly restrained by a ship's officer, and were taken off in the fourth and last lifeboat to leave. The captain and remaining crew members tried to reach a lifeboat on the aft deck, but were driven back by flames. They fashioned two rafts out of hatch covers and deck gratings that were pulled out of danger by lifeboats.

The wooden steamer became a blazing inferno. Flames ignited the deckhouses and swept up the rigging and masts. Passengers later reported that they heard explosions on board the burning ship as they sat in lifeboats waiting for rescue. They concluded that it was the munitions cargo being set off by the flames.

A tug and schooner responded to the distress flares and rescued the 65 men, women, and children. There were no fatalities or serious injuries in the loss of *Delaware*. The following morning a salvage tug found the steamer still afloat and burning, despite heavy morning rains. The tug took the burning hulk in tow, but *Delaware* sank about two miles off Bay Head, NJ.

The cause of the fire was never established. There was speculation that the two Cuban passengers had set the blaze to destroy the shipment of ammunition that was consigned to American armed forces fighting their countrymen in Cuba. It is a reasonable possibility, lacking any other evidence.

The Dive. *Delaware* is a popular dive site because it can be found with land ranges, and is accessible to divers when offshore winds make sea conditions hazardous for wrecks farther offshore.

The single screw-propeller is still fastened to its shaft. Very little of the wood hull is left in the stern. The bow, which sports a large anchor, is more intact, sitting upright with a slight list to starboard. Most of the wreckage does not extend more than five feet off the bottom. The engine is the highest point on the wreck, extending about 15 feet off the bottom. Visibility averages 15 feet, but is often very poor depending on the current, which can be very strong.

Artifacts. The personal property of passengers and crew went down with the ship. I.P. Ward of Augusta, GA, had decided to return from

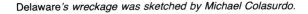

Delaware's wreckage was sketched by Michael Colasurdo.

the deck to his stateroom for his suitcase containing a gold watch, a diamond bracelet, and a set of diamond studs he had purchased in New York. But by that time, the passageway was so dense with smoke it was impassable, and the suitcase was lost.

The wooden ship was fastened with bronze spikes and pins, which are occasionally recovered by divers. More bronze fastenings are found in the bow because they joined planks to beams more securely than those of iron; the bow bears the brunt of punishment from plowing into heavy seas.

Indian Head pennies and other coins, a variety of old bottles, and brass whale-oil lamps are among the varied artifacts found by divers. In 1989, Bill Davis, an author/diver from Pennsylvania, uncovered the ship's bell on a small piece of wreckage off the main section. The 28-pound bronze bell is engraved with the ship's name and date of construction. George Hoffman, captain of the dive charter boat *Sea Lion* out of Brielle, NJ, with 32 years experience diving *Delaware*, notes that the best way to find artifacts on this wreck is to search for dark areas of sand that appear undisturbed.

Mohawk

Approximate depth: 80'
Average visibility: 25'
Expertise required: Intermediate
Current/surge: Slight to moderate
Bottom: Sand and gravel
Location: 8 miles southeast of
  Manasquan Inlet
Loran numbers: 26878.0(.1)
  43439.9 (40.0)

Launched: 1926
Sunk: January 24, 1935
Cause: Collision
Type: Passenger liner
Length/beam: 402'/54'
Tonnage: 8,140
Condition: Widely scattered
  wreckage

History. Most maritime collisions involve ships traveling in opposite directions. An outstanding exception occurred on January 24, 1935, when the passenger liner *Mohawk* was rammed and sunk by the Norwegian freighter *Talisman* 4½ miles off Bay Head, NJ.

Mohawk sailed from her East River pier in New York at 4 p.m., bound for Havana, Cuba. She passed Sandy Hook 1½ hours later. The steel-hulled liner had accommodations for 350 passengers, but only 53 were booked for the passage. She had a crew of 110, and carried about 1,300 tons of miscellaneous cargo.

The freighter *Talisman* left her New York pier at 5 p.m., an hour behind *Mohawk*. She passed Sandy Hook two hours later, bound for Delaware to pick up additional cargo. *Mohawk* should have been more than 25 miles ahead by the time the slower freighter reached Sea Girt.

The passenger liner Mohawk *was rammed and sunk by the Norwegian freighter Talisman.* Courtesy of Bill Davis, author/diver.

However, after passing Sandy Hook, the liner had lost almost two hours calibrating a new compass. It was then that the Norwegian freighter passed her.

Mohawk, built for the Clyde Line in 1926 at a cost of about $2 million, was making her first voyage for the Ward Line. Both lines were operated by the Atlantic, Gulf & West Indies Steamship Lines. The past five months had been disastrous for the Ward Line's New York to Havana run. *Mohawk* was replacing the liner *Havana*, which had run aground on a Bahamian coral reef three weeks earlier. Four months earlier, the line's pride, *Morro Castle*, had been destroyed by fire, with 24 lives lost. Tugs were still at work removing her burned-out hulk from the waters off Asbury Park, NJ.

Sinking. The temperature was five degrees above zero and the night air was completely free of fog when, at 9:37 p.m., *Talisman* rammed into the side of the liner. Survivors of the *Morro Castle* disaster claimed that the heavy loss of life could be attributed to the delay in sending out an SOS. There was no delay this time; within two minutes, wireless operators were sending distress calls from both ships. Help was not long in coming. Two steamers and a salvage tug operating in the vicinity quickly responded. The tug had been working on the removal of *Morro Castle*'s remains from nearby Asbury Park, a bitter pill for the disaster-plagued owners to swallow.

Talisman had suffered a damaged bow, but she was in no danger of sinking. A few of her starboard bow steel hull plates had been loosened and bent slightly. She was shipping only a little water. *Mohawk*, on the other hand, was listing badly and filling rapidly with the seawater that poured through a gaping hole in her port side.

Mohawk's captain, Joseph Wood, attempted to beach his damaged ship. Six years earlier, the liner had been rammed by the steamer *Jefferson* about three miles off the New Jersey coast in heavy fog. She was badly damaged and ran for shallow water where she grounded near Seabright, NJ, with 83 passengers aboard. The liner had survived that collision, but this time her engine room was flooded and the attempt to ground her was abandoned.

128

The rescue vessels played searchlights on the liner as she lowered her lifeboats. The moonlit drama continued for about two hours until *Mohawk* disappeared under the surface in 80 feet of water.

Two days after the disaster, *Talisman*'s captain, Edmund Wang, blamed the collision on *Mohawk*. He claimed that his freighter was headed south when he and his second officer observed the liner a mile or two behind, overtaking the freighter on her starboard side. *Mohawk* soon came abreast then drew ahead. As the liner moved ahead, she veered sharply to port across *Talisman*'s bow. Captain Wang ordered the freighter's engines reversed and her helm cut hard to starboard, but too late to prevent her steel bow from cutting into *Mohawk*'s port bow about 45 feet from the stem. The liner's momentum swung the freighter around to the east and the vessels parted almost at once. *Mohawk* turned toward shore with the freighter following the severely damaged liner.

Robert Barnett, a seaman on *Mohawk*'s bridge, reported that the steamer's mechanical steering device "went haywire," causing the ship to swing hard over to port. Men were ordered below to engage the hand steering apparatus, but by then the freighter's stem had cut into the liner's forecastle. A board of inquiry placed blame for the accident on *Mohawk*'s faulty steering apparatus.

Forty-five of the 163 passengers and crew were lost in the disaster, including Captain Wood, who was last seen on the bridge. The Ward Line paid $360,000 in claims for personal injuries, death, and loss of cargo. The Norwegian owners of *Talisman* contributed another $17,500.

The wreck was blown apart with explosives and wire dragged until there was a clearance of 50 feet over the site, to eliminate its threat to navigation.

The Dive. Average visibility is about 25 feet, but swells from offshore storms can quickly reduce that to zero. It is easy for divers to become disoriented in the midst of the scattered steel plates and beams and have difficulty returning to the anchor line. Ascent in a strong current without the anchor line can lead to a dangerous, exhausting swim back to the boat.

Mohawk is one of the most popular dive sites off the New Jersey coast. It is also one of the largest, scattered over about 300 yards. The most intact part is the bow, which lies on it side and projects 20 feet off the bottom. An anchor rests in the sand nearby. Three large boilers dominate the scene amidships.

The scattered steel plates and beams of the passenger liner provide divers with an excellent source of lobsters, as well as targets for spear-fishing.

Artifacts. The liner's cargo included 100-pound ingots of tin, each worth $150 at the time. During the 1960s, sport divers recovered many of them. China and silverware embossed or engraved with the Clyde Line

Artifacts recovered from Mohawk. *Photo by Michael deCamp.*

flag are found by patient divers who dig for them in the sand. They are helped by winter storms that occasionally shift the sand for them.

In 1985, following Hurricane Gloria, Kevin Brennan of Bradley Beach, NJ, discovered an area that yielded about 800 pieces of china. The china was white with a green border, and was part of *Mohawk*'s mixed cargo. Each piece of china had the manufacturer's, W.H. Grindley Co., mark on the back. In 1986, many sugar bowls, cups, and saucers with the Clyde Line's insignia embossed on them were also recovered. In addition, sterling silver tableware and serving trays engraved with "Clyde Steamship Co." were recovered. In May 1991, Captain George Hoffman, of the charter boat *Sea Lion*, and 12 other divers recovered more than 800 pieces of white china with a blue rose pattern, part of the cargo and also manufactured by the W.H. Grindley Co. Using a different dive boat, Brennan recovered about 950 pieces of the china.

Maurice Tracy

Approximate depth: 70'
Average visibility: 15'
Expertise required: Intermediate
Current/surge: Slight to moderate
Bottom: Sand
Location: 9 miles northeast of Barnegat Inlet
Loran numbers: 26889.8(90.2) 43356.9

Launched: 1916
Sunk: June 17, 1944
Cause: Collision
Type: Collier
Length/beam: 253'/43'
Tonnage: 2,468
Condition: Scattered, low wreckage; stern partially intact

(continued on page 139)

Large wooden beams from the collier Kenosha, *which sank in 1909. Photograph by the author.*

Kenosha*'s partially buried anchor was later recovered by Larry Listing and Steve Bielenda. Photo by the author.*

The passenger freighter Delaware*'s large anchor lies in the sand in the bow. Photo by Kevin Brennan.*

A school of bait fish swim over Delaware*'s disintegrating starboard boiler, in the foreground. The steamer's engine is in the background. Photo by Kevin Brennan.*

131

The first divers to visit the freighter Pinta *could easily read her name and port on her stern. Photo by Michael deCamp.*

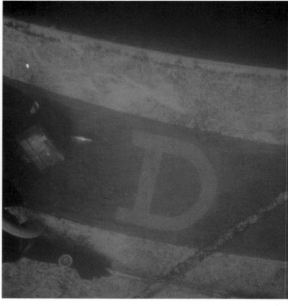

A diver inspects the yellow letter "D," which stands for the Dovar Line, on Pinta's *smokestack, five months after she sank. Photo by Michael deCamp.*

A diver grasps a control wheel for one of Pinta's *winches. Photo by Michael deCamp.*

The remains of the freighter Arundo's helm were still on the wreck in 1991. Photo by Tom Packer.

A diver inspects a train locomotive wheel, part of Arundo's cargo. Photo by Michael deCamp.

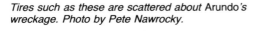

Tires such as these are scattered about Arundo's wreckage. Photo by Pete Nawrocky.

A storm cover partially covers an open porthole inside Stolt Dagali. Photo by Tom Roach.

A diver examines a ladder on the tanker Stolt Dagali's stern. Photo by Michael deCamp.

Inside one of Stolt's companionways. Photo by Brad Sheard.

Harry Augustine grasps a rocker arm on the top of Stolt's engine. Photo by Brad Sheard.

Artifacts recovered from Stolt. Photo by Tom Roach.

134

A postcard of the Clyde Line's Mohawk *at night off Jacksonville, FL. Courtesy of Bill Davis.*

A sea bass hovers over a Mohawk *porthole backing plate. Photo by Kevin Brennan.*

A partially buried porthole rim in Mohawk's *wreckage. Photo by Pete Nawrocky.*

Silver and china recovered from Mohawk. *Photo by Michael deCamp.*

The freighter Tolten'*s screw-propeller, separated from the shaft, is rigged with steel cables and is ready to be raised, September 1975. Photo by Michael deCamp.*

A lobster hides beneath a shelf containing a case of Sunlight soap bars inside the tug Great Isaac, *and one of the bars of soap recovered from the wreck. Photos by Steve Gatto.*

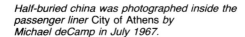

Half-buried china was photographed inside the passenger liner City of Athens *by Michael deCamp in July 1967.*

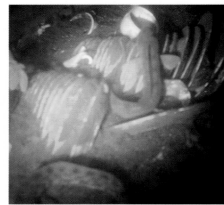

Eelpouts have taken up residence beneath two of the tanker Gulftrade's steel plates and in openings in the end of a boiler. Photos by Michael deCamp.

A cage light and a porthole in Gulftrade's wreckage. Photos by George Power.

Tom Roach photographed, recovered, and preserved this telegraph from the tanker R.P. Resor.

An alarm gong bell in Resor's stern. Photo by Steve Gatto.

The collier Maurice Tracy *was lost in a collision. Courtesy of Joe Milligan.*

(continued from page 130)

History. While the collier *Maurice Tracy* (ex. *Nordstrand*, ex. *Sekstant*) was under charter to the War Shipping Administration during World War II, she was involved in two collisions. She survived the first in March 1942, when she was rammed by the U.S.S. *Alabaster*. Two years later, a second collision proved fatal.

Sinking. On the morning of June 17, 1944, *Maurice Tracy* was en route from Portland, ME, to Norfolk, VA, with a full load of coal. At 3:45 p.m., the collier was steaming at eight knots about seven miles off Barnegat Light without her navigational lights. The blackout was a security measure against U-boats, but it contributed to her being rammed amidships by the freighter *Jesse Billingsley*. There were no fatalities, but the collier sank three hours after being struck.

The wreck was deemed to be a navigational hazard and was demolished with explosives. Now she lies in 70 feet of water.

The collier's helm was recovered in the early 1960s. Photo by Michael deCamp.

139

The Dive. The stern is partially intact and carries a deck gun that is somewhat difficult to recognize. The boilers extend up about 12 feet from the bottom. Visibility is not very good.

Artifacts. Divers have recovered the helm, anchor, and many portholes. Kevin Brennan, of Bradley Beach, NJ, has recovered five portholes. A machine-gun mount is easily recognized, but the gun has fallen into the sand and is buried.

Tolten

Approximate depth: 95'
Average visibility: 25'
Expertise required: Advanced
Current/surge: Slight
Bottom: Sand and gravel
Location: About 16 miles from both Manasquan and Barnegat inlets
Loran numbers: 26815.9 43360.1

Launched: 1938
Sunk: March 13, 1942
Cause: Torpedo
Type: Freighter
Length/beam: 280'/43'
Tonnage: 1,858
Condition: Fore and aft sections are relatively intact

History. A frequent American newspaper headline during the early months of 1942 was "Enemy submarines have struck again in home waters." One of those losses was the Chilean freighter *Tolten*. The fact that she was a neutral did not spare her from falling victim to Germany's *U-404* in March 1942, just outside New York Harbor. The freighter was not only flying the Chilean flag, but she also bore the flag of her nation painted on her hull. Her neutrality was easily recognized during daylight hours. After sunset, her navigation lights illuminated the Chilean flag as protection against attack by either side. Chile and Argentina were the only two Latin–American countries that had not severed diplomatic relations with Germany.

In 1940, after the low countries of Europe had been overrun by the German Blitzkrieg, five Danish steamers were taken over by the Chilean government for the duration of the war. *Lotta*, a freighter that had been launched in 1938, was one of the five. Her name was changed to *Tolten* after her seizure. She was the first Chilean ship sunk in World War II; her loss brought the full significance of the war to Chile. Her foreign minister summoned the German ambassador to the ministry of Foreign Affairs to protest the sinking, an incident that contributed to the emergence of a pro-Allies Chilean government.

Sinking. The Chilean freighter had discharged her cargo of nitrates at Baltimore on March 12, then sailed in ballast for New York. A U.S.

The Danish freighter Lotta *was taken over by the Chilean government during World War II. Eventually her name was changed to* Tolten. *Courtesy of the U.S. Coast Guard.*

Navy patrol vessel intercepted her around midnight and ordered all running lights extinguished. The Navy's concern was that U-boats would trail illuminated ships through mine fields protecting coastal harbors. Unfortunately for *Tolten*, running in the dark deprived her of identity as a neutral vessel.

Kapitänleutnant Otto von Bulow, commanding *U-404*, was searching for prey near the entrance to New York Harbor when he sighted *Tolten*, halfway between Barnegat and Manasquan inlets. In 1975, the German commander responded to an inquiry from scuba diver/author Tom Roach of Philadelphia with the observation that the freighter was "completely blacked out in the very dark night." Not able to identify the target's neutrality, he fired a torpedo. The resulting explosion ripped the freighter's steel hull open, and she sank within six minutes.

The only survivor from *Tolten*'s crew of 28 was the ship's electrician. When the torpedo struck, he made it from his cabin to the deck, then was "thrown clear of the sinking ship and managed to grab a loose life raft." He lost consciousness after he climbed aboard. A Coast Guard vessel rescued him twelve hours later. The only other crew member who survived the disaster was one who had been left behind in Baltimore because he missed the sailing time.

Kapitänleutnant von Bulow's 1975 letter to Roach expressed regrets at the consequences of his action against *Tolten*. "I am sorry to learn," he stated, "that only one man of the ship's crew could be saved and 27 men lost their lives and this almost in sight of the near coast." He continued, "The tremendous detonation following the torpedo hit was amazing and quite unusual. . . . " The magnitude of the explosion convinced von Bulow that his victim was carrying explosives. He was not far off the mark, although the freighter's holds were in ballast at the time. The nitrate cargo that had been unloaded in Baltimore could be used to produce either fertilizer or explosives. The residue of that cargo may have contributed to the destructive force of the explosion.

U-404 sank two more ships before von Bulow headed her back to Germany: the collier *Lemuel Burrows* off Atlantic City, NJ, and a British tanker off the coast of Maryland. On her return to American waters in the summer of 1942, the U-boat sank several more ships off North

Carolina. *U-404*'s career ended abruptly the following summer when she was sunk in the Bay of Biscay by Allied aircraft. Her commanding officer was Oberleutnant zur See Schonberg; von Bulow had by then been transferred to another U-boat command.

The Dive. On August 29, 1964, members of the Eastern Divers' Association (EDA) became the first sport divers to visit *Tolten*'s remains. One of them, Mike deCamp, noted in his dive log that the visibility was 50 feet, and both bow and stern were relatively intact. He added that the wreck, in about 95 feet of water, was "spectacular."

The president of EDA, Tom Roach, stated in a 1973 *Skin Diver* article: "The twisted, tangled maze of steel girders and plates amidships was unbelievable. The torpedo literally had blown the whole center section of the ship into oblivion. The unfortunate . . . crew must have never known what happened when that torpedo contacted the side of their ship. Everything in that section was so badly destroyed that it took a vivid imagination to try to identify what something was — or originally had been."

Tolten's bow rests in sand on its starboard side in approximately 95 feet of water. It and the stern, which has a slight list to port, are still fairly intact. They rise about 20 feet off the bottom. The wreck has many openings for penetration, and divers frequently explore the ship's corridors and compartments. What remains of her superstructure lies off in the

In September 1964, a diver grasps Tolten*'s emergency helm on the freighter's stern. Photo by Michael deCamp.*

142

sand. The site is excellent for spearfishing and gathering lobsters. *Tolten* is recognizable as a ship, rather than the junkpile of scattered wreckage that many shipwrecks resemble.

Artifacts. The ship's massive bronze, three-bladed screw-propeller was found buried in the sand. Roach commented, "it was very hard to pass that prop without the dollar signs lighting up in our eyes, but it would have been almost criminal to remove anything for salvage that could evoke the feeling of awe that propeller did. It was almost magnificent in its grave at the bottom of the sea." However, not everyone felt the same emotions. On a subsequent trip to the wreck, the EDA divers found the prized screw-propeller attached to a large lift bag. They punctured the bag, and the propeller plunged back to the bottom, where the divers took photographs and recorded the Loran numbers of the location. The respite was only temporary. The prop disappeared when persistent salvagers returned to claim their prize.

As of this writing, a spare steel screw-propeller still remains in the flattened wreckage, just forward of the intact stern section. Digging in the sand, near the bow, will occasionally produce china.

Charlemagne Tower, Jr.

Approximate depth: 55'
Average visibility: 8'
Expertise required: Intermediate
Current/surge: Moderate to extreme
Bottom: Clay
Location: About midway between Barnegat Inlet and Seaside Park, NJ
Loran numbers: 26921.8 43339.2

Launched: 1888
Sunk: March 6, 1914
Cause: Foundered
Type: Ore carrier
Length/beam: 255'/40'
Tonnage: 1,825
Condition: Flattened, low wreckage; the engine rises 25' off the bottom

History. The 26-year-old ore carrier *Charlemagne Tower, Jr.* was launched in 1888. By 1914 she was owned by the Southern Steamship Co.

Sinking. On March 6 the steamer was en route from Norfolk to Boston with a cargo of coal, when "her bottom seams opened." She foundered off the New Jersey coast in about 55 feet of water. The 17-man crew survived, but only after enduring a fierce snowstorm in a lifeboat for nearly 12 hours.

The bulk-ore carrier Charlemagne Tower, Jr. *foundered off New Jersey in 1914. Courtesy of the Steamship Historical Society Collection, University of Baltimore Library.*

The Dive. The wreck's wooden hull has broken up and flattened out, rising only a couple of feet off the bottom. The engine, which rises about 25 feet off the bottom, boiler, and other scattered machinery are in the stern.

Charlemagne Tower is also known as the "Cedar Creek Wreck," because the wreck lies offshore from where Cedar Creek flows into Barnegat Bay.

Artifacts. The wreck is not a very productive site for artifacts.

Gulftrade

Approximate depth: Bow — 55'; Stern — 85'
Average visibility: Bow — 15'; Stern — 25'
Expertise required: Bow — Intermediate if there is no surge and visibility is good; Stern — advanced
Current/surge: Slight to moderate
Bottom: Sand
Location: Bow — 4½ miles southeast of Barnegat, NJ; Stern — 13 miles east northeast of Barnegat Inlet

Loran numbers: Bow — 26886.9(9.2) 43260.6; A piece of the bow — 26894.0 43263.0; Stern — 26820.5(1.3) 43318.2(.3)
Launched: 1920
Sunk: March 10, 1942
Cause: Torpedo
Type: Tanker
Length/beam: 423'/59'
Tonnage: 6,776
Condition: Bow — flattened wreckage; Stern — intact

History. By 1942, Germany's U-boats had come perilously close to their objective of controlling the major sea lanes of the Atlantic. Sinkings of Allied ships soared to 1,570 for a total of 7,697,000 tons. Germany's *U-123* alone sank six ships in 24 hours, contributing to the loss ratio of 40 Allied ships sunk to one U-boat destroyed during the first quarter of 1942.

Winston Churchill wrote in *The Second World War*: "The Battle of the Atlantic was the dominating factor all through the war. Never for one moment could we forget that everything happening on land, sea, and in the air depended ultimately on its outcome and amid all other cares we viewed its changing fortunes day by day with hope or apprehension."

During the 1942 period of euphoria for German submarine crews, Kapitänleutnant Vogel in *U-588* headed for American waters. His orders were to stem the flow of war materials from the U.S. to her allies. Britain desperately needed fuel for her mechanized weapons in North Africa. Germany's U-boat commanders actively sought tankers as preferred targets.

Sinking. On March 10, 1942, the Gulf Oil Corporation tanker *Gulftrade* was off the New Jersey coast, en route from Port Arthur, TX, to New York with 81,223 barrels of fuel oil. Three lookouts were on the bridge and the visibility was good. It was almost 1 a.m. An hour earlier the tanker's running lights and masthead light had been turned on despite Navy regulations for all ships to run blacked out as a precaution against U-boats. A rough sea was running and Captain Torger Olsen did not want to chance a collision with one of the several colliers that were reported to be in the area. The presence of the Coast Guard cutter *Antietam*, only 300 yards away, gave Olsen false assurance of safety. He later stated

The tanker Gulftrade *was torpedoed and sunk by* U-588. *Courtesy of The Peabody Museum of Salem.*

that his ship was off Barnegat and "I thought they shouldn't be able to get us now . . . I made a mistake."

Kapitänleutnant Vogel waited patiently in *U-588*. He had no interest in the small colliers; he wanted a better target, one that he found in *Gulftrade*. He was delighted that the tanker's navigational lights were on; that made firing resolution much easier. Only one torpedo was needed. It struck just aft of the bridge, completely cutting the 22-year-old steel-hulled tanker in two. Decks were wrenched up and three tank compartments were opened to the sea. The tanker was engulfed in flames 100 feet high, but they were quickly quenched by the high seas rolling over the two partially submerged sections.

Vogel surfaced his U-boat for a calm assessment of the damage he had inflicted on the tanker, while the Coast Guard cutter vainly sought to locate the marauder. He circled the stern section as seven survivors who had remained on the stern and nine others were being rescued by *Antietam*. He even fired a torpedo at the Coast Guard vessel. It passed within 20 feet of the cutter's bow.

Sixteen men survived the disaster, less than half of the 34-man crew. The U-boat escaped in the darkness, but four months later Vogel and *U-588* were destroyed by depth charges in an attack on a North Atlantic convoy.

The torpedo cut the tanker Gulftrade *in two. The bow section, shown here, drifted until it grounded in about 55 feet of water. Courtesy of the National Archives.*

The Dive. The tanker's two halves came to rest about ten miles apart. The bow section drifted until it grounded in about 55 feet of water, approximately six miles from Barnegat, NJ, where it was visible from shore. The stern sank in about 85 feet of water approximately 13 miles east-northeast of Barnegat Inlet.

Some of the fuel oil was salvaged from the bow section before the Army Corps of Engineers attempted to blow it apart to eliminate it as a potential navigational hazard. That was proven a wasted effort when a tanker struck the wreckage in 1950, severely damaging her hull, although she remained afloat. The Corps of Engineers returned with explosives, leaving the wreckage that now projects about 12 feet off the bottom. The scattered wreckage conceals many lobsters.

Unlike the bow, the stern was not demolished. It is relatively intact, siting upright and rising about 30 feet above the bottom. Only an advanced wreck diver should penetrate the corridors and compartments, and then only with caution. The superstructure rests in sand off the starboard side. Like the bow section, the stern is good for gathering lobsters. By late summer large mussels are in abundance, a culinary treat for divers and for the large blackfish, which make this a great spot for spearfishing.

Artifacts. Divers find more artifacts, such as portholes, in the stern than in the bow. However, the remaining portholes are buried in the sand.

Cornelius Hargraves

Approximate depth: 80'
Average visibility: 20'
Expertise required: Intermediate
Current/surge: Slight to moderate
Bottom: Sand
Location: 8 miles east of
   Barnegat Inlet
Loran numbers: 26854.8
   43296.7(.9)

Launched: 1889
Sunk: October 30, 1890
Cause: Collision
Type: Schooner
Length/beam: 211'/45'
Tonnage: 1,332
Condition: Mostly covered by sand

History. The four-masted schooner *Cornelius Hargraves* was built in Camden, ME, and was owned by her captain, J.F. Allen.

The schooner's short life was filled with misfortune. She lost her anchor starting out from Camden on her first trial run. Her maiden voyage resulted in severe damage when she struck a floating wreck off the New Jersey coast. Part of her rigging was lost in a gale on her next trip. Problems plagued the unfortunate schooner even while she was in port; she was

The schooner Cornelius Hargraves *was lost in a collision with the liner* Vizcaya. *Courtesy of Bill Davis, author/diver.*

The schooner was identified when Jon Hulburt recovered this capstan cover. Photo by the author.

stranded in mud while tied up at a coal dock. She was even blown out to sea on her final voyage to Philadelphia, where she loaded a cargo of coal for delivery to Fall River, MA.

Sinking. The double-decked schooner was 13 months old when she sank in a collision with the passenger liner *Vizcaya*. Both ships were lost; they now rest on the bottom, about 150 yards apart. *Cornelius Hargraves* carried a full cargo of coal when she rammed the liner. The circumstances of the disaster are described in the *Vizcaya*'s story.

The Dive. The remains of the wooden-hulled collier were identified in August 1975 when Jon Hulburt, a newly certified wreck diver from Wilmington, DE, recovered a bronze capstan cover engraved with the ship's name.

Most of *Cornelius Hargraves* is buried under the sand bottom in about 80 feet of water. The wreck is considered a good lobster dive.

Artifacts. Deadeyes have been recovered by digging in the sand, but few artifacts are found today. Most divers prefer to dive the close-by *Vizcaya*, which produces many artifacts, such as silver serving trays.

Vizcaya

Approximate depth: 80'
Average visibility: 20'
Expertise required: Intermediate
Current/surge: Slight to moderate
Bottom: Sand
Location: 8 miles east of Barnegat Inlet
Loran numbers: 26854.6 43295.2
Launched: 1872

Sunk: October 30, 1890
Cause: Collision
Type: Passenger liner
Length/beam: 287'/38'
Tonnage: 2,458
Condition: Flattened, scattered wreckage; the engine rises 30' off the bottom

History. The Spanish passenger liner *Vizcaya* had been built in London in 1872 by J.W. Dudgeon and christened *Santander*. Her name was changed to *Vizcaya* when she was purchased by the Compania Transatlantica Española several years before her sinking.

Vizcaya was steam-powered but, like other early liners, her deck also carried masts for auxiliary sails. The sails not only reflected lack of full confidence in the steam engines; they also provided more economical transportation than the fuel-fed steam engines.

Sinking. *Vizcaya* left her New York dock at 1 p.m. on October 30, 1890, bound for Cuba and Central American ports. On board the iron-

When the Spanish passenger liner Vizcaya *was lost in a collison, only 24 crewmen of the 93 aboard, including passengers, survived. Courtesy of Bart Malone.*

hulled steamer were 16 passengers, 77 officers and crew, and a general cargo worth $35,000, including wine, scales, lumber, and stationary. By about 8 p.m. that night, the liner was off Barnegat, NJ. It was dark, but visibility was good.

At the same time, the four-masted schooner *Cornelius Hargraves* was also passing off Barnegat. She was carrying a load of coal from Philadelphia to Fall River, MA. The schooner's second mate, Angus Walker, was on deck at the time. He could clearly see what proved to be *Vizcaya*'s navigational lights about five miles away. He felt no concern because his schooner's lights were also gleaming through the night. Walker became uneasy as the two vessels came closer together; he was afraid that the steamer was unaware of the schooner. When the gap continued to close, he called Captain John Allen on deck. Allen scanned the steam-powered liner under her set of sails; he then checked the sails of his own ship and found them all set. He dismissed the problem with the remark, "I guess we can clear him."

The steamer continued on her course until Walker exclaimed, "We'll strike them, captain!" Allen swore and finally acknowledged, "Yes, we will. Hard aport, hard aport there!" His schooner rammed the liner amidships on her starboard side, almost cutting her in two. Then the schooner rebounded clear of the liner, but her billowing sails forced her into the

150

steamer again. It was a glancing blow this time, but her bowsprit swept down the steamer's deck, tearing away rigging, lifeboats, the bridge, deckhouses, and deck fittings clear to the stern.

Vizcaya began to settle at once. Five minutes later, before any lifeboats could be launched, she was on the bottom in about 80 feet of water. The schooner followed in less than a minute, but her crew managed to launch one lifeboat before she went down.

All of the liner's passengers were lost. One woman came on deck with her small boy in her arms shortly after the collision. She stumbled toward the steamer's chief engineer and shrieked, "For God's sake, save my little one." He reached out for the child, but before he could grasp him, the deck tilted as the liner started to sink. The engineer could barely save himself by lunging for a grip on the rigging. He survived. The woman and her child drowned.

Captain Francisco Cunill was on the bridge with *Vizcaya*'s third officer at the time of the collision. Both were killed by the schooner's bowsprit as it swept along the steamer's deck. Passengers in the saloon and smoking room rushed on deck after the collision. Many jumped aboard the schooner as she slid along the liner after the second impact. They were hopeful that she was not damaged as severely as the steamer. Others jumped overboard and grasped whatever floating debris they could find to keep afloat.

Captain Allen was in the schooner's wheelhouse when *Vizcaya*'s passengers and crew jumped aboard his vessel. He commanded second mate Walker to keep them back, and look after the schooner's crew first. He then ordered, "To the boats men, to the boats." The captain cut away a lifeboat with an axe, jumped in, and was followed by the rest of the crew except for Walker. The lifeboat could have held more survivors with no problem. Walker, left behind for some reason, climbed the rigging and pleaded, "For God's sake, come back." Allen's response could not be heard; he waved his hand in farewell.

Walker pushed a large gangplank over the side, jumped into the water, and climbed on top of it. Those who had transferred from *Vizcaya* abandoned the schooner as she went down. Thirteen Spaniards from the liner swam to Walker's large plank and climbed aboard. A large swell upset the plank and all aboard tumbled into the sea. When the plank righted only seven were left. After another wave, only five remained. From then on, exhausted men dropped into the water one by one until Walker was the only one left. He was rescued 11 hours after the disaster.

At about 8 a.m. the steamer *Humboldt* arrived on the scene. One of the men on watch noticed two sets of masts sticking out of the water. As the steamer drew closer a dozen men were seen clinging to the foremast yard of one vessel. The men were so cramped and stiff from their 12-hour ordeal they had to be lifted into *Humboldt*'s lifeboats. They were four officers and eight crewmen from *Vizcaya*. About 25 men had climbed into the rigging. All but a dozen of the water-soaked men succumbed to the cold and exhaustion. As they tired, or their fingers numbed, they dropped from the rigging to their deaths.

Ten men from *Cornelius Hargraves* and six from the liner who had made it to the schooner's lifeboat were rescued by the schooner *Sara L. Davis*. A pilot boat rescued Walker and six of the steamer's crew. All had been clinging to floating debris. The entire crew of the schooner survived. There had been 93 aboard *Vizcaya*, and only 24 survived, none of them passengers.

Captain Allen later stated that, as a sailing vessel, his schooner had the right of way and "it was not her place to get out of the way of the steamer. It was the steamer's duty to keep out of our way, and this is what she failed to do."

A black whistle buoy was placed over the wrecks to warn other vessels of the navigational hazard. In January 1891, explosive charges were lowered to the decks of the two ships and placed at the base of their masts. The charges were cast-iron cylinders, three feet long and one foot in diameter, each packed with 100 pounds of gunpowder. The explosive charges, called torpedoes, each weighed 325 pounds. The boats were rowed a safe distance away, and the charges were exploded by electric current through a wire attached to each charge.

The Dive. *Vizcaya* is also known as the "Spanish Wreck." Her remains are scattered over the bottom, with only the bow, engine, and boilers projecting any distance above the sand.

A small wooden fishing boat sank in the middle of *Vizcaya*'s iron hull plates; divers often mistake the wooden wreckage as part of the Spanish passenger liner.

A silver tray and silver dish after being cleaned by George Power. The steamship line's insignia is engraved in the center of each. Photo by the author.

A silver encased shaving mug and brush recovered by George Power. Photo by the author.

152

George Power with three silver trays he recovered from the passenger liner. Courtesy of George Power.

Artifacts. The wreck has produced many artifacts; in recent years some of the steamer's china and silverware, bearing the steamship's line insignia, have been recovered. A box of jewelry and gold coins were also found. The ship sank so quickly that passengers and crew were unable to save their personal belongings. Among the passengers were two of Cuba's wealthiest families.

Divers using underwater scooters have worked the wreck successfully during winter months by reversing their scooters and using the prop wash to clear sand away from submerged artifacts. In 1991, George Power, of Magnolia, NJ, recovered a solid bronze chandelier and several silver trays with the steamship line's insignia engraved in the center.

R.P. Resor

Approximate depth: 130'
Average visibility: 40'
Expertise required: Advanced
Current/surge: Slight
Bottom: Sand
Location: 31 miles east of Barnegat Inlet
Loran numbers: 26638.3 43277.1
Launched: 1936

Sunk: February 28, 1942
Cause: Torpedo
Type: Tanker
Length/beam: 435'/66'
Tonnage: 7,451
Condition: Flattened wreckage amidships; the bow and stern are relatively intact

History. Winston Churchill wrote in *The Second World War*: "Battles might be won or lost, enterprise succeed or miscarry, territories might be gained or quitted, but dominating all our power to carry on the war, or even keep ourselves alive, was our mastery of the ocean routes and free approach and entry to our ports." It is widely recognized that wars

153

The tanker R.P. Resor *was torpedoed by* U-578. *Courtesy of the Steamship Historical Society Collection, University of Baltimore Library.*

are not won exclusively by tankers and freighters, but wars can be lost without them. Subscribing to that truism, German U-boats hunting in U.S. waters took an appalling toll of merchant vessels during World War II. Their primary targets were tankers — and *R.P. Resor* was a tanker.

Sinking. A solitary U-boat, *U-578*, under the command of Korvetten-kapitän Rehwinkel, lurked off the New Jersey shore in the early morning of February 27, 1942. She was stationed to pounce upon any likely victim just as the Standard Oil Company tanker *R.P. Resor* neared completion of her run from Baytown, TX, to Fall River, MA.

The tanker was loaded with 78,729 barrels of crude oil, and she was armed with a 4-inch gun on her stern. She was 18 miles off the New Jersey coast, completely blacked out and steaming a zigzag course. The weather was fine, sea calm, moon up, and visibility good. Three lookouts were on the alert for U-boat activity, but more attention was devoted to the starboard, seaward side of the vessel. It was expected that any attack, if it came, would be from the deep-water side.

In a bold move, Captain Rehwinkel had surfaced his U-boat inland of the tanker and turned on his running lights as he moved into firing position. As he had hoped, the tanker's crew mistook the submarine for a friendly fishing vessel. They were unaware that they were under attack until two torpedoes struck the tanker's port side. There were four explosions, two from the torpedoes, the third and fourth from the oil-laden hold.

The sensational fire provided a grim spectacle for early risers along the New Jersey shore. They watched as flames soared 200 feet skyward through the night. The sun rose upon a massive black pall of smoke along the horizon. The burning tanker drifted southeast for nearly two days before she sank approximately 31 miles off shore in about 130 feet of water.

There were only two fire-scarred and oil-coated survivors from the crew of 49, which included eight Navy gunners. A Coast Guard vessel arrived at the scene and pulled close to the blazing tanker in response to cries for help, but blinding smoke and intense heat foiled their efforts. They withdrew, with the paint on their boat beginning to blister. Efforts were then concentrated on picking up survivors.

John Forsdal, one who lived through the ordeal, had been on lookout duty. He later reported that he had seen running lights on what he thought was a fishing vessel, then sounded two bells, warning the bridge that the vessel had been sighted two points off the port bow. Forsdal gave no further thought to the unidentified boat until the first torpedo struck, throwing him into the air and knocking him unconscious for several seconds. When he regained consciousness, the entire aft section of the tanker was aflame. He dropped a life raft over the side, but by the time he lowered himself down a line, the raft had drifted off into the sea. His frantic search was rewarded when he found it with the ship's radio operator clinging to its side. Both were completely coated with thick oil that frustrated their efforts to climb aboard. After a desperate struggle in the cold, oily water, they both managed to haul themselves onto the raft.

The tanker's cargo of 78,729 barrels of oil fed the raging fires, and the billowing clouds of smoke could easily be seen from shore. Only two members of the 49-man crew were rescued. Courtesy of the Submarine Force Library and Museum.

The Coast Guard boat threw a rescue line that Forsdal clutched but lost as he was pulled off and away from the raft. He made his way back, but the radio operator was no longer there, nor was he ever seen again.

The only other survivor, Daniel Hey, one of the Navy gunners, was asleep in his bunk when the torpedo struck. By the time he reached the deck, the ship was engulfed in flames, with blazing oil pouring into the sea for a distance of 500 feet. He joined three others in an effort to lower a lifeboat, but flames drove them back. They jumped into the sea and swam for an opening in the ring of fire, but Hey was the only one who managed to break through. Another lifeboat, loaded to the gunwales, pushed off from the tanker, but none of its occupants survived.

Hey pulled himself aboard a life raft and was picked up by the Coast Guard an hour and a half later, coated with a heavy layer of congealed oil that protected him from freezing in the midwinter cold Atlantic. The coastguardsmen removed his clothes by cutting them off with a knife. In addition to picking up the two survivors, they also recovered four bodies.

R.P. Resor was six years old when she was lost, the 26th ship sunk or damaged in U.S. waters in the 45 days between January 14, 1942, when U-boats began hunting off the Atlantic coast, and her February 28 sinking. Seventeen of the ships were tankers laden with war-vital oil, prime targets for the Germans. Korvettenkapitän Rehwinkel and his *U-578* crew did not survive long to savor their share of those victories. Six months after the U-boat sank *R.P. Resor*, the U-boat was lost with all hands in an attack by Allied aircraft in the North Atlantic.

The Dive. The tanker's bow, facing east-northeast, and the forward cargo tank are pretty much intact, sitting upright on the bottom. The superstructure amidships is broken up and scattered. The aft cargo tanks are flattened, but the stern, listing to the port side, is relatively intact. It extends about 35 feet off the bottom. Marine life is abundant, and the wreck lies far enough offshore that Gulf Stream waters often provide excellent visibility that averages 40 feet, but ranges as far as 60 to 70 feet.

Several openings in the stern allow access to passageways and compartments. The deck gun is still mounted on the stern, its barrel pointing down toward the sand bottom. It remains a symbol of initial American futility in the face of Nazi Germany's Operation Paukenschlag, the all-out U-boat assault on U.S. coastal shipping. In German, Paukenschlag (literally drumbeat) is a metaphor for thunderbolt, an apt description of the impact it had on U.S. commerce. It was a time known by German submariners as "the American turkey-shoot" or the "Second Happy Time." The first was against British shipping in the early days of the war.

R.P. Resor represents all those merchant vessels that were lost before convoys and air patrols brought the U-boat threat to coastal commerce under control.

The wreck is considered a good dive for lobsters and for spearfishing cod and pollock.

Artifacts. Salvors from New Jersey recovered the ship's bell before the tanker settled to the bottom. The deck gun is still attached to the stern, and at the time of this writing, at least one porthole was left.

Persephone

Approximate depth: 55'
Average visibility: 10'
Expertise required: Intermediate
Current/surge: Moderate to extreme
Bottom: Sand
Location: 3 miles east of Barnegat Inlet
Loran numbers: 26897.0(.1) 43287.0(.1)(.6)

Launched: 1925
Sunk: May 25, 1942
Cause: Torpedo
Type: Tanker
Length/beam: 468'/63'
Tonnage: 8,426
Condition: Flattened, scattered wreckage

History. During the first six months of 1942, U-boat successes in U.S. waters startled even the most optimistic of the German submarine commanders. In January 1942, 35 ships were sunk; 45 went down in February; and 76 in March. April showed a drop to 52, but the May total was 105, and June, 110. During the first half of 1942, U-boats claimed 423 merchant ships sunk in the western Atlantic. By mid-1942, American defenses had managed to sink several U-boats off the American coast, but that was little consolation for the wholesale losses of Allied merchant shipping.

By July 1942, the convoy system was in operation along the East Coast. The once lucrative Atlantic seaboard waters were no longer easy pickings for the U-boat. There, as elsewhere in the war theater, Allied counteraction had wrested the initiative from the U-boat, reversing her role from hunter to prey. The once happy days of sea domination and shooting gallery sinkings, measured in millions of tons, had come to an end.

The convoy system had been implemented as soon as escort vessels became available. However, U.S. military forces were inexperienced in escort procedures. Their ineptitude resulted in loss of the Panama Transport Company's tanker *Persephone*.

Sinking. On May 25, 1942, the Panamanian tanker was traveling in a convoy of about 20 ships extending from one horizon to the other. Most of the ships were six miles or more ahead of *Persephone* because of her slower, 10-knot speed. The 17-year-old unarmed tanker was supposedly protected by surface escorts and air cover. One of the escorts, a Coast Guard vessel, was about five miles southeast, circling the wreckage of a ship that had been hit several days earlier.

The Panamanian tanker Persephone *was torpedoed by* U-593; *her stern rests on the bottom. Two lifeboats filled with survivors can be seen, one in front of the forward mast, the other beneath the Navy blimp. Courtesy of the National Archives.*

The tanker was en route from Aruba to New York with about 80,000 barrels of crude oil. At 3 p.m. a torpedo struck her engine room; 30 seconds later a second torpedo hit the #8 tank. Both struck the starboard side. Fortunately, the ship did not catch fire, although there was a brief flash of fire when the second torpedo hit. Almost immediately, the tanker's stern settled to the bottom, leaving the bow and midship superstructure sticking out of the water.

Ten minutes later, 28 of the crew of 37 abandoned ship in a single lifeboat, a life raft, or by leaping into the sea. Captain Helge Quistgaard, last to leave the tanker, lowered a second lifeboat; he was the only occupant. Nine men below deck or stationed aft were lost. The survivors were picked up by four Coast Guard vessels. The captain returned to the tanker with several coastguardsmen and salvaged his ship's papers and 23 bags of mail.

Captain Quistgaard later protested to the Navy that "his ship was in a crude convoy. There was no uniform speed and although patrolled by a blimp and other aircraft, as well as surface vessels, the ships in the convoy were so extended as to make adequate patrol impossible."

Escort vessels and aircraft searched for the U-boat without success. Korvettenkapitän Kelbling in *U-593* had escaped, but on December 13, 1943, he encountered more experienced U.S. naval forces northeast of Algiers and *U-593* was sunk by depth charges. Kelbling and his entire crew managed to escape from the sinking U-boat. They were captured and spent the remainder of the war as prisoners.

Persephone's bow remained afloat. A salvage crew cut the ship in half and towed the forward section, which contained 20,000 barrels of oil, to New York.

Some of the crew returned to the tanker to retrieve personal belongings. Courtesy of the National Archives.

The following year the midship superstructure of the salvaged portion was removed for installation on the Esso tanker *Livingston Roe*, which had lost her own superstructure in a fire.

The Dive. *Persephone*'s stern section was blown apart with explosives and wire dragged in 1944. Today the wreckage is scattered about the bottom, but the site is good for lobsters, spearfishing, and an occasional brass artifact.

Artifacts. The wreck is not a very productive site for artifacts.

Sumner

Approximate depth: 25'
Average visibility: 10'
Expertise required: Novice if there is no surge
Current/surge: None to extreme
Bottom: Sand
Location: By Barnegat Lighthouse
Loran numbers: 26916.8 43271.7

Launched: 1883
Sunk: December 12, 1916
Cause: Ran aground
Type: Passenger freighter
Length/beam: 351'/43'
Tonnage: 3,553
Condition: Scattered wreckage, mostly covered by sand

History. Many vessels have been converted into colliers, but it is unusual for a coal carrying ship to be refitted as a passenger vessel.

The U.S. Army transport Sumner, *in Army colors, photographed at the Norfolk Navy Yard in March 1900. Courtesy of the Naval Historical Center.*

The collier *Rhaetia* was launched in 1883 as a merchant vessel. Five years later, during the Spanish-American War, the steamer was purchased by the U.S. Navy to carry coal to Cuba and renamed U.S.S. *Cassius*. After the war, the collier was refitted as a transport, and in 1899 was sold to the War Department.

Sinking. On December 12, 1916, the U.S. Army transport, by then renamed *Sumner*, was en route from Panama to New York. Just before midnight, she ran aground in dense fog by Barnegat Lighthouse. There were 232 passengers on board, mostly troops and Panama Canal civilian employees, including eleven women and eight children.

The ship grounded so lightly that most of the passengers were not awakened. One newspaper headline read "WRECK WITHOUT A THRILL."

Passengers were rescued by the Coast Guard the next morning. Two days later, after it was concluded that the ship could not be refloated, the 120 crew members were removed.

Even though the ship had grounded "lightly," the 800 tons of scrap iron she carried in her forward hold caused the bow to settle into the sand. Two salvage tugs strained to pull her off, then abandoned the effort. Salvors removed much of the iron before heavy seas broke the steel-hulled ship's back.

The Dive. Steel hull plates and other wreckage are scattered about. Most of the wreck is buried under the sand, but in some areas wreckage extends up a few feet. From year to year divers do not know how much of the wreck will be exposed or covered by the shifting sand. Visibility is usually poor. There is some disagreement as to whether the scattered wreckage is the *Sumner* or some other wreck.

Artifacts. The wreck is not a productive site for artifacts. Any remaining artifacts would be buried in the sand.

San Saba

Approximate depth: 80'
Average visibility: 25'
Expertise required: Intermediate
Current/surge: Slight
Bottom: Sand
Location: 7½ miles southeast of Barnegat Inlet
Loran numbers: Bow — 26853.8 43239.5; Stern — 26853.2 43240.6

Launched: 1879
Sunk: October 4, 1918
Cause: Mine
Type: Freighter
Length/beam: 306'/39'
Tonnage: 2,458
Condition: Two sections of flattened wreckage, fewer than 100 yards apart

History. During World War I, Germany developed large U-boats that could cross the Atlantic to harass the flow of men, munitions, and food coming from America to bolster the Allied war effort. Six of those U-boats destroyed 165,000 tons of shipping in waters along the eastern seaboard from Newfoundland to Cape Hatteras. Although that accomplished little to end hostilities in Europe, it did provide an omen of the long-range potential of the German U-boat.

In July 1918, *U-156* laid mines off the coast of Long Island; one of them sank the armored cruiser *San Diego*. Before the U-boat departed for Germany she was replaced on station by *U-117*, another mine layer that had been commissioned in late June, then headed for American waters after shakedown trials. The Germans used the new U-boat's deck gun to make their presence felt on August 10 by attacking a swordfishing fleet 60 miles east of Nantucket. Two days later, one of her torpedoes sank the Norwegian freighter *Sommerstadt* off Long Island. The following day, Kapitänleutnant Droscher and *U-117* sank the American tanker *Frederick R. Kellogg* 30 miles south of the Ambrose lightship, 11 miles off the New Jersey coast. On August 14, *U-117* sank the five-masted schooner *Dorothy B. Barrett*.

Sweeping down the coast, the U-boat deposited seven mines before continuing her marauding patrol; the mines reaped a rich harvest long after *U-117* left the Atlantic seaboard for Germany. The U.S. battleship

Minnesota was seriously damaged by one. There was no loss of life and the battleship did not sink, but she underwent five months of repairs.

The Mallory Line's iron-hulled freighter *San Saba* was launched in 1879 and christened *Colorado*. In 1915, she caught fire and was abandoned at sea. Salvage tugs towed her into port with some of her cargo of 6,000 bales of cotton still ablaze. The freighter was rebuilt and renamed *San Saba*.

Sinking. The first disaster from the seven mines laid by *U-117* came on October 4, 1918, when *San Saba* struck one off Surf City, NJ. The freighter was en route from New York to Tampa with a general cargo; she sank within five minutes. Captain B.G. Birdsall and 30 of his 37-man crew were either killed in the explosion, drowned, or died of exposure.

Seven days after striking the German mine, the freighter's bow remained afloat; her stern rested on the bottom in about 80 feet of water. The bow was deemed a navigational hazard and was sent to the bottom with Coast Guard cutter gunfire. The freighter broke into two pieces that settled fewer than 100 yards apart.

On October 27, the Cuban freighter *Chaparra* hit one of the U-boat's mines and sank in less than three minutes. The final sinking of the war in American waters occurred just two days before the Armistice — another *U-117* mine victim. She was the army cargo carrier U.S.S. *Saetia*, sunk on November 9, 1918. The German U-boat was responsible for sinking 23 vessels between August 10 and November 9, for a total of 35,020 tons.

The freighter San Saba *struck a mine laid by* U-117. *Courtesy of The Peabody Museum of Salem.*

The Dive. The bow of *San Saba* is a hardly recognizable mass of iron hull plates. A pile of anchor chain rises from the midst of the scattered debris. A large boiler is forward in the stern section. The ship's screw-propeller is still attached to its shaft.

Artifacts. A variety of artifacts are recovered from the freighter's general cargo, including .22 caliber ammunition and five-pound ingots of babbitt metal, an alloy of tin, copper, and antimony. The ingots are stamped "Magnolia antifriction metal." For that reason, some divers refer to *San Saba* as the "Magnolia Wreck."

Chaparra

Approximate depth: 80'
Average visibility: 25'
Expertise required: Intermediate
Current/surge: Slight
Bottom: Sand
Location: 8½ miles southeast of Barnegat Inlet
Loran numbers: 26847.6 43239.9

Launched: 1906
Sunk: October 27, 1918
Cause: Mine
Type: Freighter
Length/beam: 249'/38'
Tonnage: 1,510
Condition: Flattened hull plates and scattered wreckage

History. As October 1918 drew to a close, the end of World War I was only two weeks away, but Germany's U-boats remained a constant threat to merchant shipping along the Atlantic seaboard of the United

The freighter Chaparra *struck a mine laid by* U-117, *only 23 days after* San Saba *was sunk by one. Courtesy of The Mariners' Museum, Newport News, VA.*

States. Their torpedoes, deck guns, and mines had taken a heavy toll of ships, lives, and cargoes. No seaman knew whether his ship would be the next to be victimized by a U-boat. *U-117* had combined torpedo and deck gun actions with the laying of seven mines along America's seaboard. Her mines had already claimed one victim, the Mallory Line freighter *San Saba*, earlier in the month (see pages 145-147).

Sinking. The Cuban freighter *Chaparra* was en route from Havana to New York on October 27, 1918, with a cargo of sugar when she struck another of *U-117*'s mines. The sugar-laden freighter sank in less than three minutes. Germany's 200-pound mines carried a devastating charge of destruction.

Captain Jose Vinslas reported that the mine detonated just forward of the bridge on the port side. An awesome explosion lifted the 1,510-ton freighter out of the sea with an accompanying column of water that erupted over the bridge. Twenty-three men quickly abandoned ship in two lifeboats; six went down with the freighter. After rowing for 22 hours, the survivors reached shore at Barnegat Light, so exhausted that they had to be half-carried into the keeper's cottage.

The Dive. The wreck lies on her port side; the iron hull plates in the stern are flattened. The midships area is a jumbled mass of tangled debris. The bow, however, extends a few feet above the bottom.

Her remains abound in lobsters, as well as providing divers ground for good spearfishing.

This deck light was recovered from Chaparra *by Evelyn Dudas. Deck lights were laid flush into the deck with the prism pointing into the cabin below so that sunlight would be dispersed through the prism. Photo by the author.*

Artifacts. Artifacts are occasionally recovered, but the wreck does not produce the variety of items that are found around *San Saba*. *San Saba* carried a general cargo. *Chaparra*'s holds were filled only with sugar, a fragile commodity when immersed in 80 feet of seawater.

Great Isaac

Approximate depth: 90'
Average visibility: 20'
Expertise required: Intermediate to advanced
Current/surge: Slight to moderate
Bottom: Sand and silt
Location: 10 miles south southeast of Barnegat Inlet

Loran numbers: 26840.9 43195.2
Launched: 1944
Sunk: April 16, 1947
Cause: Collision
Type: Tug
Length/beam: 185'/37'
Tonnage: 1,117
Condition: Intact

History. The oceangoing tug *Great Isaac* was built during World War II. She was named after a lighthouse in the Bahamas. The tug was owned by the Maritime Commission and was under lease to the Moran Towing and Transportation Company.

Sinking. On April 16, 1947, *Great Isaac*, with a crew of 47, was towing a Liberty ship from Norfolk, VA, to New York when she encoun-

The oceangoing tug Great Isaac *was almost twice the size of a harbor tug. The nonfunctional dummy smokestack was for aesthetics only. A tarpaulin-covered 3-inch deck gun can be seen on the bow in this wartime photo. Courtesy of Bill Davis, author/diver.*

tered dense fog off Ship Bottom, NJ. Her foghorn repeatedly sounded its warning, and her crew could hear the foghorn of another ship.

The Norwegian freighter *Bandeirante* was en route from New York to Cuba. Her captain later reported that he did not hear the tug's foghorn. When *Bandeirante* loomed up on *Great Isaac*'s port side, the tug was hampered from taking evasive action by the tow line attached to the Liberty ship. The Norwegian freighter's bow cut six feet into the tug's engine room. No lives were lost, but the ocean tug sank.

The Dive. *Great Isaac* lies intact on her port side. The wreck is partially buried, but still extends up about 20 feet off the bottom.

It is possible to penetrate the wheelhouse, engine room, crew's quarters, and several hatches. Ambient light enters through rusted-out holes in some areas of the steel hull. However, disturbed silt will reduce visibility, even in those areas. Divers can become disoriented within the wreck, particularly because the tug is on her side. Extreme caution is essential for any diver entering the wreck.

Great Isaac is a good site for finding lobsters.

Artifacts. A few portholes on the starboard side have not been recovered. The portholes on the port side are buried under about ten feet of sediment. The wreck is not a prolific source of artifacts, but they are occasionally recovered from the sunken oceangoing tug.

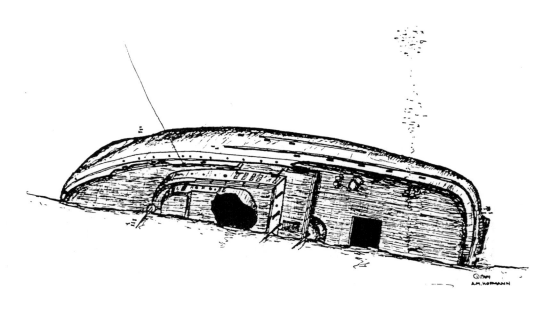

Great Isaac's *wreckage was sketched by Al Hofmann.*

Approximate depth: 65'
Average visibility: 20'
Expertise required: Intermediate
Current/surge: Slight to moderate
Bottom: Sand
Location: 8½ miles east of
Absecon Inlet
Loran numbers: 26918.0 43025.7

Launched: 1909
Sunk: September 6, 1918
Cause: Collision
Type: Passenger freighter
Length/beam: 378'/50'
Tonnage: 3,121
Condition: Scattered wreckage

History and sinking. The United Fruit Company's passenger freighter *Almirante* was en route from New York to Colon, Panama, in dense fog on the night of September 6, 1918, when she was rammed by the 15,000-ton U.S. Navy tanker *Hisko*. The tanker cut deeply into the smaller, nine-year-old passenger freighter. Luckily, only seven passengers and 98 crew were on board. Five crew members were lost.

Almirante sank in about 65 feet of water and was blown apart twice with explosives, then wire dragged to decrease her potential as a navigational hazard. The ship's primary cargo of flour washed ashore at Brigatine, NJ, fouling the beach for weeks and identifying her as the "Flour Wreck."

The passenger freighter Almirante *was lost in a collision in 1918. Courtesy of Bill Davis, author/diver.*

A postcard showing the interior of the passenger freighter's stateroom #6. Courtesy of Bill Davis.

The Dive. *Almirante* sank while World War I was still in progress. During the Second World War, her remains were mistakenly identified as a U-boat and depth charged, further scattering the wreckage that today provides an ideal source of lobsters and artifacts.

Artifacts. Brass door locks, large valves, several portholes, a telegraph, and the ship's helm have been recovered. However, china and the ship's bell have not been found, and many portholes are still buried in the sand.

Lemuel Burrows

Approximate depth: 80'
Average visibility: 20'
Expertise required: Intermediate
Current/surge: Slight to moderate
Bottom: Sand
Location: 8 miles southeast of Absecon Inlet
Loran numbers: 26928.2 42991.1
Launched: 1917

Sunk: March 14, 1942
Cause: Torpedo
Type: Collier
Length/beam: 437'/63'
Tonnage: 7,610
Condition: Broken up, but some areas extend a good distance off the bottom

History. Nazi Germany's Kapitänleutnant von Bulow was in command of *U-404* when he torpedoed the Chilean freighter *Tolten* off Seaside Park, NJ, on March 13, 1942. The following day he followed up by sinking the American collier *Lemuel Burrows*. But in the process, he used three torpedoes. That was an unprecedented overkill, the first time a U-boat had expended that many torpedoes on a single ship in American waters. Why he found it necessary is not known.

Torpedoes were as precious a commodity as fuel in determining how long a U-boat could stay on patrol. During the First World War, U-boat deck guns could, and did, dispatch enemy merchant ships to the bottom. During World War II, airplanes and their antisubmarine weapons tended to keep German submarines submerged, with less opportunity to bring deck guns into action. When a U-boat had expended all her torpedoes she headed for home.

At the time of her sinking, *Lemuel Burrows* was owned by the Eastern Gas and Fuel Associates. Her previous owner had christened the collier *Deepwater* when she was launched in 1917.

Sinking. The *Lemuel Burrows* was doomed by *U-404*'s first torpedo; her captain ordered abandon ship. The second struck while two lifeboats were being launched. One of the lifeboats was destroyed by the detonation, so two life rafts were pushed over the side. The third torpedo struck amidships, lifting the collier into the air. When she settled back, the resulting wave overturned the lifeboat that had been launched, throwing survivors into the sea. They held onto the overturned lifeboat and the two rafts, but not all made it. When rescue arrived six hours later, only fourteen had survived the ordeal. Twenty died in the disaster.

Sixteen months later, *U-404* was sunk by U.S. Army aircraft off the coast of France, but without von Bulow. Command of the U-boat had by that time been turned over to his former executive officer, Oberleutnant zur See Shonberg.

The freighter Lemuel Burrows *was torpedoed by* U-404. *Courtesy of Joe Milligan.*

The Dive. The three torpedoes that sank *Lemuel Burrows* tore the ship apart. Then the hazard to navigation was wire dragged twice, the last time to a depth of 39 feet. The harsh treatment she received left the wreck a jumbled mass of steel beams and plates, but some sections still protrude a good distance above the bottom. *Lemuel Burrows* is a large wreck that is a good site for artifacts, lobsters, and spearfishing. It is often referred to as the "Collier."

Artifacts. In 1990, several large brass letters from the ship's name were recovered from the bridge area. Brass valves, gears, and other mechanical items can be found in the remains of the engine room.

San Jose

Approximate depth: 110'
Average visibility: 10'
Expertise required: Advanced
Current/surge: Moderate
Bottom: Silt and mud
Location: 14 miles southeast of Absecon Inlet
Loran numbers: 26877.5 42955.4

Launched: 1904
Sunk: January 17, 1942
Cause: Collision
Type: Passenger freighter
Length/beam: 330'/44'
Tonnage: 3,358
Condition: Basically intact

History. On January 17, 1942, United Fruit Company's passenger freighter *San Jose* was en route to New York. The U.S. had been at war for little more than a month, but U-boats were already operating in American waters. A U-boat had sunk the tanker *Norness* off Block Island on January 14, and the tanker *Coimbra* off Long Island the following day. Those losses prompted the U.S. Navy to order ships to run without navigation lights to mask their movements from marauding U-boats.

Sinking. As *San Jose* steamed north off the southern New Jersey coast, the passenger freighter *Santa Elisa* was headed south on her maiden voyage. It was about 8 p.m., with both ships blacked out as ordered; neither carried passengers. Off Atlantic City, the new *Santa Elisa* rammed the 38-year-old *San Jose*. The collision left a gaping gash in the new ship's port bow. The damage did not put her in danger of sinking, but it did ignite the barrels of oil that were part of her cargo.

As *Santa Elisa*'s crew fought the flames, *San Jose*'s crew abandoned their ship. The 3,358-ton steamer's starboard hull had been deeply pierced by the steel stem of the much larger, 9,758-ton ship. Several seamen were injured, but there were no fatalities. Three steamers responding to the distress calls rescued 40 men in *San Jose*'s lifeboats.

The passenger freighter San Jose *was rammed and sunk during the Second World War. Courtesy of the Steamship Historical Society Collection, University of Baltimore Library.*

Santa Elisa burned through the night, and until around noon the following day. When the flames were extinguished she was towed to New York and repaired.

San Jose was not considered worth the time or cost to salvage. She had been launched in 1904, 38 years earlier. In 1950 the wreck, already heavily damaged by collision, was blown apart with explosives and then wire dragged to eliminate her as a navigational hazard.

The Dive. *San Jose* is partially intact, from midships back, lying on her port side, in about 110 feet of water. Many sections project as much as 20 feet above the bottom, and large masts lie in the sand. Although visibility is often bad, the scattered wreckage is a good source of artifacts, and contains many niches for lobsters.

Artifacts. In 1990, a brass builder's plaque, about 12 feet by 20 feet, from the refrigeration equipment, was recovered. The crest of the manufacturer, Shipley Co., was engraved on it. Remnants of large glass carboys can been seen under steel plates amidships. Complete carboys may be buried in the sand. Portholes are still buried in the sand, and none of the bridge equipment has been recovered as of this writing.

Dorothy B. Barrett

Approximate depth: 60'
Average visibility: 15'
Expertise required: Intermediate
Current/surge: Moderate
Bottom: Sand
Location: 20 miles south of Great Egg Inlet
Loran numbers: 26963.4 42773.1

Launched: 1904
Sunk: August 14, 1918
Cause: Gunfire
Type: Schooner
Length/beam: 259'/45'
Tonnage: 2,088
Condition: Flattened wreckage usually covered by sand

With her deck gun, U-117 *sank the schooner* Dorothy B. Barrett. *Courtesy of The Mariners' Museum, Newport News, VA.*

U-117 *was brought to America as a war prize after the First World War. She was sunk by aerial bombardment off Cape Charles, VA, after extensive U.S. Navy testing. Courtesy of the National Archives.*

History. *U-117*, under command of Kapitänleutnant Droscher, made a mark for herself and Imperial Germany's efforts to throttle commerce along the Atlantic seaboard late in World War I. The U-boat was commissioned in June 1918; by August, the new U-boat was making her presence felt in American waters with her torpedoes, mines, and deck gun. Those exploits are covered in more detail in the story of *San Saba*, starting on page 161.

The German U-boat survived World War I, then was turned over to the United States after hostilities ended. By agreement, Germany's U-boats were made available to the victors only for technical study, training, and public display, not for active naval service. On July, 22, 1921, a U.S. training exercise sank the war prize by aerial bombardment, 50 miles east of Cape Charles, VA, beyond the 50-fathom line.

Sinking. The 14-year-old five-masted schooner *Dorothy B. Barrett* was one of *U-117*'s victims, but not by mine or torpedo. The schooner was en route from New York to Norfolk when *U-117* fired a warning shot across her bow. After Captain William Merritt and his crew of ten were granted the opportunity to abandon ship, the vessel was sunk by the U-boat's deck gun.

The Dive. The flattened wreckage is usually covered by sand. Storms and current occasionally uncover parts of the World War I wreck, and then the site is a good lobster dive.

Artifacts. Deadeyes and brass belaying pins have been recovered in the past, but more artifacts are probably buried in the sand.

City of Athens

Approximate depth: 110'
Average visibility: 40'
Expertise required: Advanced
Current/surge: Moderate
Bottom: Sand
Location: 26 miles south of Great Egg Inlet
Loran numbers: 26920.1(.3) 42705.3(.4)

Launched: 1911
Sunk: May 1, 1918
Cause: Collision
Type: Passenger liner
Length/beam: 390.1'/46.2'
Tonnage: 3,648
Condition: Hull is collapsed; scattered wreckage

History. Historical statisticians estimate that the First World War was responsible for the deaths of almost ten million men and women. Excluded from such estimates are those who died during the war under noncombat conditions, but as an indirect result of the conflict. These included the 67 passengers of the passenger liner *City of Athens*, sunk in 1918 in a collision with a friendly Allied warship.

The success of Germany's unrestricted submarine warfare had transformed the United States from contemplative, if biased, neutral to an active belligerent, hostile to Germany. American military personnel and supplies were urgently needed in Europe if the Kaiser's invaders were to be turned back. That meant transporting men and materials across the Atlantic against the constant threat of U-boats. Convoys with American, British, and French warships as escorts provided a solution to that problem.

The steamer *City of Athens* had been launched in 1911 as *Somerset* for the Merchants & Miners Transportation Company of Savannah. In September 1917, the six-year-old passenger liner was acquired by the Savan-

The passenger liner City of Athens *(ex.* Somerset*) was sunk in a collision in 1918. Courtesy of Bill Davis, author/diver.*

nah Line's parent company, the Ocean Steamship Company of Savannah. Her name was changed to *City of Athens*, and she was then placed on the New York to Savannah run.

Sinking. On May 1, 1918, only six months before the "Great War" ended, the French armored cruiser *La Gloire* was en route to New York Harbor in fog off the southern New Jersey coast, under orders to provide escort for a convoy bound for Europe.

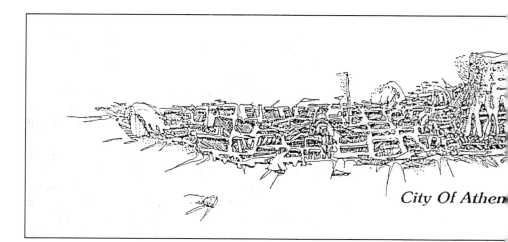

City Of Athen

The coastal passenger liner *City of Athens* of the Savannah Line was feeling her way south through the fog, headed for Savannah, GA, with 137 passengers and crew. All deck lights and ports were blacked out because of heavy U-boat activity in American coastal waters. Her navigation lights were on, but they would serve little use if the deepening fog worsened.

About an hour past midnight, the French warship and the American passenger liner were 26 miles off the New Jersey coast. Their foghorns blared warning signals, and deck watches had been increased. Captain A.C. Forward, commanding the merchant vessel, later wrote that fog signals of an approaching vessel could be heard, but that the exact location could not be determined. Suddenly the steel bow of the 10,000-ton warship loomed out of the fog, almost dead ahead. It cut through the side of the smaller liner like a meat cleaver, striking the starboard bow at the anchor and penetrating to the navigating bridge.

The gaping hole in the passenger ship's bow provided easy entry for in-rushing seawater as the liner was carried forward by her own momentum. She sank in seven minutes, carrying half of those on board with her. All passengers and many of the crew were asleep when the collision occurred. Despite the shock of the impact, many in the stern of the passenger vessel failed to realize how serious the situation was until it was too late.

Most of the passengers rushed on deck; women and children were hastily loaded aboard lifeboats. One of the boats capsized as it was being lowered to the sea when a rope broke. The liner sank so quickly that some of the lifeboats could not be lowered. The passengers and crew

The liner's wreckage was sketched by Greg Modelle and Charles Cole.

who remained on deck were swept into the moderately rough sea as the vessel sank. Some lifeboats close to the sinking ship were capsized by the wave that was produced as the liner went under.

The French warship's bow was severely damaged by the force of the collision, but there was no loss of life and she was in no danger of sinking. She stood by and lowered her boats at once in search of survivors. Although hampered by fog, the warship's searchlights managed to illuminate those clinging to floating debris or struggling in the water. In an ironic twist of fate, 14 of the 69 who perished were French sailors who were *City of Athens* passengers. They were part of a contingent of 20 French seamen who had been sent to the United States to replace crews of French antisubmarine patrol vessels. They had been quartered in the bow, where their nation's cruiser sliced into the passenger liner's hull.

There were American military casualties as well. On board the liner were 24 U.S. Marine recruits assigned to Port Royal, SC, for basic training. Seven were drowned. One 19-year-old marine who was awakened by the collision later recalled, "I jumped out of bed . . . and shook my partner in the bunk above . . . and told him he had better hurry. Somehow I could not make him understand. He just rubbed his eyes, yawned, and wanted to turn over and go back to sleep again. I learned later that he was drowned."

The young Marine rushed on deck. When he realized how badly the boat was listing, he decided not to try to board a lifeboat. Instead, he slid down a pole to the deck below and prepared to leap off the rail. The decision was taken away from him when a tremendous wave piled over the side and swept him overboard. When he surfaced, he was looking directly into the eye of a searchlight. As he swam toward it, he reached a French sailor who was holding himself afloat by holding onto a box. The language problem was overcome when the Frenchman nodded his head and the American gained a hold on the floating debris. The French sailor's "Sauve! Sauve!" calls for help drew response from the French warship; one of its boats picked up the two survivors.

Recovery of the ship's bell, inscribed with the name Somerset *and the launching date 1911, identified the wreck. Photo by Smokey Roberts.*

The wreck is also known as "the good bottle wreck" because of the variety of bottles recovered. These are a few recovered by Bart Malone. Photo by the author.

A passenger from Mobile, AL, was the first to be taken aboard the French warship. She anxiously waited for news of her husband, from whom she had been separated by the order of "Women and children first." She learned later that he had drowned.

Two women and one four-year-old child were among the missing; three other women were seriously injured. The liner's radio operator, F.J. Doherty, who had remained at his station to transmit calls for help, was one of the 69 passengers and crew who perished. Survivors totaled 35 passengers and 33 members of the crew, just fewer than half of those aboard when the collision occurred.

The Dive. Very little of the wreck is intact today. The hull has collapsed and is scattered in about 110 feet of water. The highest points are the ship's two boilers. Visibility is usually very good, averaging 40 feet and often exceeding 50.

Artifacts. Portholes, bottles, china, silverware, and many other artifacts typical of an early 20th-century passenger liner are occasionally recovered. The ship's general cargo included cases of rifles and small arms ammunition for French patrol vessels. Divers have recovered thousands of 8mm La Belle cartridges with the date and arsenal clearly marked, which is why the site is affectionately referred to as the "Ammo Wreck." It is also known as the "26 mile wreck" because of its distance from the New Jersey shore.

In 1991, china was recovered by digging in the sand in front of the boiler.

177

Approximate depth: 25'
Average visibility: 5'
Expertise required: Advanced because of the very strong current
Current/surge: Extreme
Bottom: Sand
Location: Sunset Beach, Cape May, NJ
Loran numbers: Not needed; the wreck extends above the surface

Launched: 1918
Sunk: June 1926
Cause: Stranded
Type: Freighter
Length/beam: 260'/43'
Tonnage: 2,500
Condition: Concrete hull in very deteriorated condition

History. The steel shortage that prevailed during World War I led to the construction of ferroconcrete-hulled freighters. The U.S. Shipping Board placed orders for 40, but only 12 keels were laid before the Armistice ended the war. One of those that went into production was *Atlantus*. She was launched on December 4, 1918, less than a month after the war ended.

Atlantus's heavy, five-inch-thick, steel-reinforced-concrete hull made her slower and less efficient than conventional steel-hulled vessels. The freighter made several transatlantic crossings over the period of a year before she was mothballed at Norfolk, VA. The New Jersey-Delaware

The concrete freighter Atlantus. *Courtesy of the Steamship Historical Society Collection, University of Baltimore Library.*

A postcard of Atlantus *as a hulk at Cape May; note the sign on the bow advertising boat insurance. Courtesy of Bill Davis.*

Ferry Co. purchased *Atlantus* in 1926, intending to sink her and fill her hull with sand, to serve as a breakwater and dock on the Cape May, NJ, side of the Cape May–Lewes, DE, ferry.

Sinking. The concrete ship was stripped, towed to Cape May, and anchored off Sunset Beach on June 8, to await the dredging of her permanent site. About midmonth a storm blew her aground and she could not be refloated.

The Dive. The concrete hull has broken up over the years, but sections still extend about 15 feet above the surface. The dive site is near the mouth of the Delaware River; extreme tidal currents have to be considered when planning a dive.

The wreck is easily accessible from shore, but tidal changes must be monitored. Only strong swimmers should attempt to dive this wreck, and even then they should head back to shore before the current intensifies. Steel reinforcing rods extend out of the concrete hull, posing a hazard for divers entering the water from a boat. They project upward just beneath the surface, with steel tips sharpened into spearheads by the oxidization of rods that once were blunt.

Artifacts. This wreck is not a very productive dive for the collection of artifacts.

4

Dive Procedures and Safety

Most shipwrecks off the New York/New Jersey coast require access by boat. For those without their own boats, dive charter boats are listed on pages 184-185. Some charter boats allow walk-on passengers on the day of a dive; others require advance booking. The U.S. Coast Guard has established rigid safety regulations for all passenger-carrying vessels, requiring that the boat's license and the captain's license be prominently displayed. Divers are cautioned to ensure that their dive charter boat displays a U.S. Coast Guard license, and that the vessel is not loaded beyond the number of passengers it is certified to carry. The boat should be stocked with an adequate first-aid kit and oxygen to handle emergencies.

If the captain or a member of the crew does not mention water entry and exit methods, ask. If a current is running, do not hesitate to request a current line (a line extending from the boat's stern to the anchor line). Some dive charter boats exceed 50 feet in length, and swimming against a strong current is tiring. Avoid straddling the current line when entering the water. A trail line with a float should be off the boat's stern for the diver who is carried past the ladder by the current. The line may also be used by divers waiting their turn to climb the ladder after a dive.

In diving from a private boat, always leave someone aboard who is capable of operating the boat and its communication equipment in case of emergency. Buddy diving is essential whether diving from a boat or the beach, and a dive flag is required by law. Unfortunately, too many pleasure-boat operators either do not know what a dive flag represents or they ignore it. Be aware of passing boat traffic at all times.

When diving in poor visibility or on a large wreck, a tether line should be tied near the bottom to the anchor line, to be reeled out as the diver explores the shipwreck. The tether line should be reeled in as the diver returns to the anchor line. Never cut the tether line at the end of a dive to avoid the time it takes to reel it in. Lines left on the bottom are a potential entangling hazard for others. It is much safer to ascend the anchor line after a dive than to surface away from the dive boat, where the diver could be struck by another vessel, or be confronted with a tiring swim against a strong current.

Most divers entering the interior of a wreck use a penetration line (a line tied near the entrance and reeled out as the diver swims into the

180

wreck). It can be followed back to the entrance when the diver is ready to exit. A diver who cuts the line at the furthest penetration point to avoid rewinding is endangering those who follow by leaving an entangling hazard behind.

Swim against the current while exploring the wreck if there is a current on the bottom. The current will then aid return to the anchor line.

Redundancy of equipment is important — especially air supply. A backup system such as a pony bottle or double tanks with separate regulators is important. Two means of checking both depth and bottom time should be part of a diver's equipment. Often only a dive computer is used; if it should fail, a diver will have no record of depth or time unless he or she carried a bottom timer and depth gauge. A *sharp* knife is mandatory for diving shipwrecks because of the entangling monofilament from fishermen and the nets of trawlers. Two knives should be included in case one is lost while entering the water or during the dive. In addition, two lights are needed if penetration is part of the dive plan; the battery or bulb could fail, or a light could flood. Backup equipment is especially important for wreck penetrations, and wreck penetrations are for advanced divers only. Only you know your limitations — *dive within them.*

The Divers Alert Network (DAN), a membership association of individuals and organizations sharing a common interest in diving safety, operates a 24-hour national hotline — (919) 684-8111 (collect calls are accepted in an emergency). DAN does not directly provide medical care. However, the network does provide advice on early treatment, evacuation, and hyperbaric treatment of diving-related injuries. Additionally, DAN provides diving safety information to members to avoid accidents. Membership of $10 a year offers:

- The DAN *Underwater Diving Accident Manual,* which describes symptoms of, and first aid for, major diving-related injuries.

- Emergency room physician guidelines for drugs and I.V. fluids.

- A membership card listing diving-related symptoms on one side and DAN's emergency and nonemergency phone numbers on the other.

- A tank decal and three small equipment decals with DAN's logo and emergency number.

- A newsletter, *Alert Diver,* which describes diving medicine and safety information in layman's language, with articles for professionals, case histories, and medical questions related to diving.

The DAN manual can be purchased separately for $4, and membership applications can be obtained from: Administrative Coordinator, National Diving Alert Network, Duke University Medical Center, Box 3823, Durham, NC 27710. DAN's nonemergency telephone number is (919) 684-2948.

Appendix

The list below is included as a service to the reader. The author has made every effort to make this list complete at the time this book was printed. This list does not consitute an endorsement of these operators and dive shops.

Local Dive Stores

New York

#1 Dive Inc.
1 South Central Ave., Valley Stream
(516) 872-4571

AAA Richards Aqua Lung Ctr.
233 W. 42nd St., New York
(212) 947-5018

Ador-Aqua
42 West 18th St., New York
(212) 645-1234

Allen Sport Shop
249 North Ave., New Rochelle
(914) 235-3430

Aqua Crazy Harvey
3179 Emmons Ave., Brooklyn
(718) 743-0054

Byram Bay Sports
500 North Main St., Port Chester
(914) 937-2685

Captain Mikes
634 City Island Ave., Bronx
(212) 885-1588

Central Skindivers
160-09 Jamica Ave., Jamaica
(718) 739-5772

Danny's Dive Shop
2150 Grand Ave., Baldwin
(516) 223-8989

Diving-Adventures Into Our World
1152 Broadway, Hewlitt
(516) 374-7756

Dive Locker
621 E. Boston Post Rd., Mamaroneck
(914) 381-5935

Divers Way
596 Sunrise Hwy, Bayshore
(516) 665-7990

The Dive Shop
RD 4 Box 11 Rt. 32, New Windsor
(914) 534-8515

The Diving Center
26 Wolcott Rd., Levittown
(516) 796-6560

Dutchess Diving Ctr.
503 South Rd. Rt. 9, Poughkeepsie
(914) 462-0255

East Coast Diving
1500 Hylan Blvd., Staten Island
(718) 979-6056

The Enchanted Diver
259-19 Hillside Ave., Floral Park
(718) 470-6858

Fantasea Ski & Scuba
2510 Hylan Blvd., Staten Island
(716) 667-3232

Hudson River Scuba Sales
RD 3 Box 3A, Rt. 44, Pleasant Valley
(914) 635-3488

Innerspace Dive Shop
57 Forest Ave., Glen Cove
(516) 671-5454

Island Scuba
74 Woodcleft Ave., Freeport
(516) 546-2030

Kings County Divers
2417 Ave. U, Brooklyn
(718) 648-4232

Lone Star Diving School
20 W. 22nd St. #612, New York
(211) 989-6831

Marsh Scuba Supply
19 Lauer Rd., Poughkeepsie
(914) 452-8994

Martini Scuba
2037 Central Park Ave., Yonkers
(914) 779-9786

Middletown Scuba
17 Dolson Ave., Middletown
(914) 343-2858

Midhudson Diving Ctr.
Boices Ln., Kingston
(914) 336-5333

Pan Aqua Diving
166 W. 75 St., New York
(212) 496-2267

Paragon Sports
871 Broadway at 18th St., New York
(212) 255-8036

Port Diver Scuba Ctr.
811 Rt. 25A, Port Jefferson
(516) 331-9609

Putnam Dive Ctr
Rt. 6 N., Mahopac
(914) 628-1386

Regional Divers
326 N. Plank Rd., Newburg
(914) 566-1112

Scuba Network
1 Park Row, New York
(212) 571-1800

The Scuba Shoppe
428 South Country Rd., Brookhaven
(516) 286-5552

Scuba Training & Equip. Ctr.
12 Bobby Lane, West Nyack
(914) 358-6250

Scuba World
167 W. 72nd St., New York
(212) 496-2220

Sea Scapes Dive Ctr.
737 A Smithtown Bypass, Smithtown
(516) 366-4588

7Z's Hampton Bay's Divers
1140 Flanders Rd., Flanders
(516) 727-2642

Sound Watersports
271 Bayville Ave., Baysville
(516) 628-3389

Suffolk Diving Ctr.
58 Larkfield Rd., East Northport
(516) 261-4388

Swim King
572 Rt. 25A, Rocky Point
(516) 744-7707

Underwater World
RD 5, Box 271 Riverside Rd.,
  Jamestown
(716) 569-5509

Westchester Dive Ctr.
Rt. 118, Mahopac
(914) 628-1386

New Jersey

Atlantic Divers
RD 3, Box 4 Fire Rd., Pleasantville
(609) 641-7722

Brielle Dive Center
428 Euclid Ave., Brielle
(908) 528-8444

Cedar Grove Divers Supply
492 Rt. 23, Cedar Grove
(201) 857-1748

Certified Scuba Divers
1546 Springfield Ave., Maplewood
(201) 378-2025

Chatham Water Sports
9 N. Passaic Ave., Chatham
(201) 635-5313

Divers Cove
Hwy 35, Laurence Harbor
(908) 583-2717

Divers Two
One Main St., Avon
(908) 776-7755

The Dive Shop of NJ
RD 1, 33 Delsea Dr., Hurffville
(609) 589-2434

Dosil's Sports Center
261 Hwy 36, North Middleton
(908) 787-0508

East Coast Diving Service
340F Spring Valley Rd., Morganville
(908) 591-9374

East Coast Diving Supply
1002 New Rd., Northfield
(609) 646-5090

The Edison S/D Center
1659 Hwy 27, Edison
(908) 985-2206

Elite Divers
Brick Church Plaza, Rt. 46, Denville
(201) 586-2214

Harbor Divers
73 Tiller Dr., Waretown
(609) 693-8999

Lakeland Divers, Inc.
92 Rt. 10, East Hanover
(201) 887-0194

Lang's Ski & Sport
106 Stanhope St., Princeton
(609) 987-8882

Marlin Scuba Center
506 Rt. 17, Ramsey
(201) 327-6000

New Jersey Scuba Supply
Market Place 1990 E. Rt. 70, Cherry Hill
(609) 751-6702

Ocean Explorers Aquatic Ctr.
871 Rt. 1, Edison
(908) 287-2822

Princeton Aqua Sports
306 Alexander St., Princeton
(609) 924-4240

Professional Divers Inc.
70 Hwy 35, Neptune City
(908) 775-8292

The Scuba Center
4237 Hwy 9, Freehold
(908) 462-4660

Scuba Network
4 Rt. 4 West, River Edge
(201) 488-7916

Sea-Sun Sports
1017 Cedarbridge Ave., Bricktown
(908) 920-7177

Triton Divers
4404 Long Beach Blvd., Brant Beach
(609) 494-4400

Underwater Adventures
1152 Rt. 10, Randolph
(201) 584-2789

Underwater Discovery
2722 Rt. 37 E., Toms River
(908) 270-9100

Underwater Sports of NJ
Rt. 17 S., Rochelle Park
(201) 843-3340

Whitehouse Aquatic Ctr.
6 Rt. 22 W., Whitehouse Station
(908) 534-4090

Local Dive Charter Boats

New York

Alania
Montauk, (516) 668-9025

Apache Jr.
Long Island Sound, (914) 965-8659

Defiance
Long Island Sound, (212) 409-2647

Diver
Huntington Harbor, (516) 261-4388

Diver One
Long Island Sound, (212) 863-8799

Eagle's Nest
Jones Inlet, (516) 735-2254

Firebird
Long Island Sound, (212) 885-1011

Jeanne II
New York Bight, (718) 332-9574

Joan "M"
Huntington Harbor, (516) 266-3312

Karen
Rockaway Inlet, (718) 373-9005

Martini Scuba
New Rochelle, (914) 779-9786

Northern Star
Fire Island Inlet, (516) 366-4231

Rebel
Rockaway Inlet, (718) 897-2885

Sea Hawk
Jones Inlet, (718) 279-1345

Sea Hunter
Jones Inlet, (516) 628-8928

Shearwater II
Fire Island Inlet, (516) 242-0529

Southern Cross
Fire Island Inlet, (516) 587-3625

Wahoo
Fire Island Inlet, (516) 928-3849

Wreck-Reation
New York Bight, (718) 840-0143

New Jersey

Anastasia
Absecon Inlet, (609) 476-2301

Blue Fathoms
Manasquan Inlet, (908) 937-7995

Captain Cramer
Hereford Inlet, (609) 368-1548

Captain's Lady
Barnegat Inlet, (609) 268-2152

Cigarette
Barnegat Inlet, (908) 859-4384

Danny's Choice
Manasquan Inlet, (201) 783-4056

Daybreak III
Manasquan Inlet, (201) 347-5341

Deep Adventures
Manasquan Inlet, (201) 270-8888

Deep Six
Manasquan Inlet, (201) 226-4477

Dina Dee
Manasquan Inlet, (201) 840-5664

Diversion
Manasquan Inlet, (201) 477-8404

Down Deep
Cape May, (609) 953-3374

Down Under
Barnegat Inlet, (609) 296-0333

Ebbie III
Absecon Inlet, (609) 646-5090

Explorer
Manasquan Inlet, (201) 946-0822

Finesse
Barnegat Inlet, (609) 693-8999

Good Times II
Barnegat Inlet, (609) 346-0687

Horizon
Absecon Inlet, (609) 628-2459

Joint Venture
Manasquan Inlet, (609) 983-8683

Lady Grace
Manasquan Inlet, (908) 892-2064

Lady Monica
Cape May Inlet, (609) 875-0677

Lauren R
Manasquan Inlet, (201) 546-0459

Linda B
Barnegat Inlet, (609) 971-0281

Robin II
Barnegat Inlet, (609) 693-7386

Sea Gull
Manasquan Inlet, (201) 223-4080

Sea Lion
Manasquan Inlet, (201) 528-6298

Seeker
Manasquan Inlet, (908) 223-1734

Ursula
Townsend Inlet, (609) 646-5090

Venture III
Manasquan Inlet, (201) 928-4519

Whitestar IV
Barnegat Inlet, (609) 494-0425

Index